The Smarter Bet Guide to Craps

Everything you need to play craps like a pro

Basil Nestor

DORSET PRESS
NEW YORK

This book is dedicated to Ron, Connie, Terry, and the rest of the gang in the Las Vegas Forum at CompuServe.

Contents

Introduction
Dice: The World's Oldest Game

Learning a new gambling game can often be an intimidating experience. Even though we're adults, the child inside us (the one who really wants to play) remembers when performance at games was tied to self-esteem. What would other people think if we did-n't know the rules? What would happen if we performed badly?

Craps is the casino contest that most often causes these feel-ings, probably because it most resembles a childhood game. Think about it. It's played at a monster-sized table with more lines and numbers than a hopscotch pyramid. It's a group game that involves many people, sometimes more than a dozen. It has a bizarre and colorful lexicon. Craps players throw something. And of course, everyone can see when you fail. This combination of psychological factors can make craps every bit as frightening to the child within us as our worst first experience playing soft-ball, freeze-tag, or soccer.

But consider this…craps, and more specifically dice as a game, is older and more universal than any of those other contests or any casino gambling game. Most games measure their history in cen-turies, but dice go all the way back to the beginning of civilization.

Something so old and familiar should hardly be the object of apprehension. Is it that the table seems complicated? Forget the table. I'll explain this in detail in Chapter 2, but right now just take my word for it; the only numbers you have to under-stand are two through twelve. Craps is entirely about the dice.

Exactly how old and ubiquitous are those cubes? If we were to magically transport an Egyptian pharaoh from Africa in 2500 B.C.E. to a modern casino 4,500 years later, the only thing he would immediately recognize would be the dice (assuming the casino was not the Luxor). Of course, the clear tinted plastic would amaze him, but the basic design of our modern cubes, six sides with values of one through six, is essentially unchanged since ancient times.

Dice in the Ancient World

In fact, dice go back even farther. Ankle bones of sheep, antelope, and other animals have been found in prehistoric digs. These were the stone-age versions of early dice. Four-sided dice and other variations persisted into classical antiquity, but cubes quickly became the gamers' favorite. And there were a lot of gamers, particularly because the nature of gambling had an entirely different significance in the ancient world than it does today. For example, the word "gamble" isn't mentioned anywhere in either Testament. That's because the concepts of random distribution and impartial results simply didn't exist for the vast majority of people who were "casting lots." It was God or "the gods" who determined the outcome of every contest. So lots were cast by Joshua to determine how the Promised Land would be apportioned, and the apostles in Acts 1:26 cast lots to decide who would replace Judas. The Jewish festival of Purim (the word means "lot" in the Semitic language of Akkadian) is based on a fateful gamble in Esther 3:7. And Saul used the two sacred stones, Urim and Thummim, to determine the guilt of his son in 1 Samuel 14:41.

Remember, this was an age when the entrails of sheep could predict a victory on the battlefield. Nothing was random in the ancient world. Everyone was casting lots.

Roman Recreation

Of course, everyone wasn't always deathly serious about their dice games, particularly hedonistic Romans. According to the historian Plutarch, Cleopatra beguiled Mark Antony with carousing, drinking, and dice. Augustus Caesar loved playing so much that he bankrolled his opponents. The Emperor Claudius wrote a book about winning at dice. Nero regularly played for 400,000 sestercia per throw, and Emperor Commodus actually had part of his palace converted to a casino to raise money for his treasury.

Dice played a metaphorical role in changing the history of the world when Julius Caesar crossed the Rubicon on his way to conquering Rome. He shouted to his soldiers, "The die has been thrown!" and thus bet his life. The entire Roman republic (soon to be an empire) was the prize.

Yes, the Romans loved gambling, but they were fickle in their affections (like so many other later cultures). Rome blamed the dice (among other things) for problems in society. Gambling was outlawed in various stages as the Empire crumbled. As usual, prohibition didn't stop the forbidden activity; it simply drove it underground, further undermining the social order.

By the early fifth century the tattered remnants of the empire were Christian, and dice had developed a particularly bad rap for their role in the crucifixion story (soldiers cast lots for Jesus' clothing). Furthermore, divination was considered to be evil in a big way. Dice and gambling were removed completely from the natural order of things and were placed squarely in the realm of vice. According to St. Augustine of Hippo, "The Devil invented dicing." God's will was not subject to choice or chance. End of discussion. A beating with rods or nasty lessons with hot tongs were frequently in store for anyone who held a different opinion.

Hazard and Craps

Medieval society perceived the cubes as dangerous. Indeed, our word "hazard" comes from the Arabic phrase for dice, *al-zahr*. Hazard began as the humble name of a dice game (the forerunner of craps), but the word eventually became synonymous with jeopardy and risk.

Hazard appeared in Palestine during the Crusades around the year 1100, and it was soon quite popular in Europe, particularly in France and England. The basic game involved rolling a point and then repeating for a win. That's identical to modern craps. The rest of the contest was much more complicated. It included "chance points," "nicks," and rules that changed when different numbers appeared. Significantly, "crabs" was a slang expression describing a roll of 2. There is no record as to how this phrase developed, but 2 was an automatic loser then as it is now. Perhaps when the dice produced something that looked like a crab's pincers people imagined a pinch on their wallets.

Hazard was clearly a big hit in the old world, but North America never embraced it. The European game was too complicated and too arcane for the unpretentious rough-and-tumble frontier. Hazard needed a facelift for the new world, and that's what it got in the early nineteenth century on the French wharves of New Orleans. Sailors and slaves replaced the difficult rules with the 7-11-point pass challenge familiar to modern players. They called the modified game "crabs." Americans who played it on the Mississippi had no idea what the French were saying. It sounded more like "craps." The moniker stuck.

And that clears up one of the most common misconceptions about craps. The name has absolutely nothing to do with Thomas Crapper or his famous invention.

Modern Craps

It was another man with a descriptive name, John H. Winn, who modified craps into the form we know today. Winn was a dice maker, and he noticed that many people avoided craps because they weren't allowed to bet against the shooter (the person throwing the dice). Players simply didn't trust one-way contests. So, in 1907 he invented the modern table layout with the **don't pass** (see Chapter 2). That allowed players to bet both sides of the proposition. Winn's contributions also include the **hardways**, **place bets**, and **vigorish** (see Chapters 4 and 5). Early craps tables were simply pool tables with a wooden rail. Chalk lines divided the betting areas.

Nice improvement, but the heart of the game was still the dice. One of the ironies of modern craps is that the game with the biggest table, the biggest crew, and the most complicated layout is actually the game that requires none of those trappings. Craps is about the cubes. That fact and the practical nature of waging war are what fueled the enormous popularity of craps during the first half of the twentieth century.

Dice are really small, even smaller than cards, and far less cumbersome. You can carry them anywhere, even on a boat, even into battle. Craps was tremendously popular with Allied soldiers and sailors during the two world wars. The game could last two minutes or all night. Any number of people could play, and the dice (and money) could disappear in a moment if a mortar shell came arcing over or the captain suddenly walked past.

That's why so many old men love the game. That's how craps got its tough-guy image and why it became the most popular casino game during the middle decades of the twentieth century.

The irony is that this enormous popularity eventually caused the game to decline as baby boomers grew up. Craps was Dad's game. Your cigar-chomping uncle threw dice. Blackjack seemed more refined. Then along came slots. By the mid '90s, craps had slipped from its prime position as the most dominant casino game to a status closer to roulette and baccarat, just a few tables bobbing in a sea of machines.

But the new millennium has given craps a boost and has again proven that it has a special vibe that sets it apart from the quieter contests. Baby boomers have finally begun to come around (perhaps prodded by generations X and Y). The Rat Pack, *Guys and Dolls*, and other dice-oriented pop culture icons have graduated from being anachronisms to retro coolness. Many experienced gamers are moving up from slots to more advantageous and challenging contests, and craps is one of the best. In fact, craps is often a better bet than blackjack (more on that in Chapter 1).

Go into any large casino on a Friday or Saturday night, and you'll see people of all ages crowded around craps tables, shouting and cheering.

So, the amazing epic continues. Dice survived the fearsome prohibitions of Rome and St. Augustine. The cubes have been carried by emperors, crusaders, and Marines. And now it's your turn.

It's the world's oldest gambling game, and you're a part of it.

You and the pharaohs, baby!

Part

Basic Craps

Chapter

Gaming:
A Crash Course

THIS CHAPTER IS *NOT* ABOUT THE RULES OF CRAPS; IT'S ABOUT the rules of the universe (otherwise known as **odds**) and how those rules relate to craps. Why do coins flip the way they do? Why do cards fall a certain way? What numbers will the dice produce? What is a good bet? How do you identify a sucker bet?

Consider the Super Bowl. Picking the winner is easy some years because one team has an overwhelming advantage. Other years it's more difficult to predict the outcome. But imagine if the season's statistics weren't available. It would be impossible to say who has an edge and who is the underdog. Wagering without the stats is a sucker bet (assuming your opponent has more information than you).

The same is true of every game, especially craps. The rules tell you how to play, but the odds and probabilities tell you who will win. Craps has good and bad wagers (as you'll soon see). You can't separate the good from the bad without knowing the stats.

Heads vs. Tails, Negative vs. Positive

Take a quarter and flip it. Will George Washington beat the eagle? There's no way to know. That's why they call it a "toss up." Neither side has an advantage. Neither side can expect to win one decision or the majority of decisions. A lucky streak could favor George, or the streak could go the other way. A streak may never appear, or there may be many streaks. Anything is possible.

If the payoff on a heads-or-tails wager is 1:1 (even money), then both players have an equal probability of turning a profit or suffering a loss. Remember, a bet requires two opposing persons or entities.

But let's say the payoff goes higher or lower (1:2, 2:1, and so on). The **true odds** are still 1:1, but the **payoff odds**, or **house odds**, have shifted. The player who is getting the extra money has a **positive expectation** and the person who is giving the extra money has a **negative expectation**. The difference could be as little as one penny on a dollar wager, but that alone would do it. There is still no way to predict who will win most of the decisions, but one side will inexorably, inevitably, and permanently win more money as the flips continue.

It's a mathematical fact, a rule of the universe. The person wagering the positive side could quit her job and retire if the other person would just consistently and rapidly keep flipping and betting. This is how casinos earn a profit. They don't have to win all the time. They don't even have to win most of the time; they just need to have a positive expectation. This advantage is commonly known as the **house edge**, and it's usually measured as a percent of the wager.

In the above example a one-penny difference in the payoff on a one-dollar coin-flip proposition translates into a one-half percent house edge (a typical bettor would be down an average of one cent after two decisions or one-half cent after one decision).

Obviously, it's impossible to lose one-half cent—a player either wins 99 cents or loses one dollar. But over time the player will lose (on average) one-half percent of all the dollars that are wagered. It doesn't sound like a lot, especially if you're lucky enough to catch a winning streak, but those giant palaces in Las Vegas and Atlantic City were built on similar minuscule advantages.

Of course, the casino is also perfectly willing to offer sucker bets with edges that soar into the teens and above. But the meat-and-potatoes wagers usually carry an edge that is five percent or less. The table "Good and Bad Casino Bets" (see page 16) gives examples of the house edge on various popular contests. The list goes from best to worst.

Notice that a game can simultaneously offer good bets and sucker bets. That is certainly the case in craps, where uninformed or reckless players can be seen shoveling money onto the worst wagers while ignoring the better ones. I'll help you separate the diamonds from the dregs in later chapters, but right now let's continue with the subject of expectation.

Who Has the Edge?

In the table "Good and Bad Casino Bets" I classify low-edge bets as "good." Of course, that's a relative term. The best bets have a positive advantage, and that's certainly better than a slim disadvantage. Unfortunately, positive-expectation wagers aren't easy to find in a casino. Most games are negative expectation for players. It's possible to shift some contests from negative to positive by using an **optimal strategy** (a mathematically optimized system of play), but doing that requires a bit of effort and considerable patience. Keep in mind that the typical advantage

Good and Bad Casino Bets

Game	Bet	Casino Advantage
Craps	Pass line with 5X odds	0.33%
Video Poker	9/6 machine with optimal strategy	0.46%
Blackjack	Using basic strategy (no counting)	0.5%
Baccarat	Banker	1.06%
Roulette	European wheel with surrender	1.35%
Craps	Pass line	1.41%
Video Poker	6/5 machine with optimal strategy	4.5%
Roulette	American wheel with no surrender	5.26%
Roulette	American wheel—five numbers (0,00,1,2,3)	7.9%
Blackjack	Insurance	8.2%
Slots	Progressive	10.0%
Baccarat	Tie	14.4%
Craps	Any seven	16.7%
Keno	Most "big board" bets	30.0%

Blackjack, slots, and keno figures are averages for typical games.

remains around one percent or less, even when it's pushed to the player's side. There is no money spigot in a casino. In fact, an often-used phrase from late-night television absolutely applies here; casinos earn money with volume, volume, volume! That's how professional players earn a living, too.

Remember, streaks happen. Jackpots hit. Even negative-expectation games are "winnable" in the short run. That's why people continue to play. It's only when you multiply the decisions into the thousands and hundreds of thousands that the house edge inevitably extracts its profit.

Some gambling purists will claim that every game has an Achilles' heel, a weakness that can be exploited for positive expectation. That's true, but only if you can get certain uncommon odds, or if you can find a particular situation. If, if, if... the world is full of ifs, but the "Long-Term Player Expectation" list (see page 18) gives you the standard expectation for most games in most casinos. If you find a craps game that pays 2:1 for naturals on the pass line, write me a letter; we'll both win millions (until the casino goes bankrupt).

In the meantime, craps is a negative-expectation contest. There is no system or strategy that can change that.

Does that mean craps players always lose? Absolutely not! What it does mean is that craps players who *play badly* almost always lose. They're paying the casino's electric bills. But you don't have to be one of them.

Long-Term Player Expectation

Here's a list of the most popular
casino games organized by expectation.

Negative Expectation	Positive Expectation
Poker (typical player)	Poker (pro)
Blackjack (without counting)	Blackjack (with counting)
Video Poker (without optimal strategy)	Video Poker (with optimal strategy)
Sports Bettor (typical player)	Sports Bettor (pro)
Baccarat	
Craps	
Let It Ride™	
Caribbean Stud Poker™	
Roulette	
Slots	
Keno	

There is a way to lower the house edge on craps to around one percent, and in some cases all the way to zero. That's essentially pushing the edge back to a 1:1 coin-flip type contest. Nobody can predict if George will beat the eagle, but at least you have a reasonable shot at winning.

Why would casinos offer such advantageous bets when it might cost them money? The answer is somewhat complex and involves public relations and marketing considerations, but it boils down to this; most people don't bother to learn the correct game strategy. It's just too much trouble. They'd rather lose. So the casinos get the PR boost of offering "100% payback" wagers, and the games still earn money.

Incredible but true.

Many craps players don't even try to lower the house edge. They just bet whatever strikes their fancy. It's an expensive convenience. The table "Cumulative Effects of the House Edge" (see page 20) shows the average expected loss of a reg-

Smarter Bet Tip
If you're interested in learning positive-expectation strategies for poker, video poker, and blackjack, check out the Smarter Bet Guides to those games.

Cumulative Effects of the House Edge

Number of Decisions	Average Loss for a Regular Player: 5% edge, $10 bets	Average Loss for an Optimal-strategy player: 1% edge, $10 bets
50	$25	$5
100	$50	$10
150	$75	$15
200	$100	$20
250	$125	$25
300	$150	$30

300 decisions is approximately three to five hours of typical craps play.

ular player who doesn't use a sound craps strategy compared to that of an average optimal-strategy player.

Of course, anything can happen. The regular player might experience an amazing streak that puts him solidly in the plus column, but consider how much less luck is required for the optimal-strategy player to turn a profit, just four winning decisions on average instead of sixteen. And it's easy to see which player will last longer if the table turns cold. Bad luck, good luck, or no luck, the optimal-strategy player will always lose less or win more in the long run.

True Odds – House Odds = Casino Profit

House odds is the payoff that is proudly listed on the sign or boldly printed on the felt of the table. True odds is the actual probability of winning (something that is rarely mentioned by a casino). As we saw with the coin flips, the difference is the house edge.

Lowering or eliminating the edge is only possible if you know where to find it. Casinos do a pretty good job of disguising their advantage, particularly in the game of craps. Sometimes they lower the payoff a smidgen, as in our coin-flip example. Other times they charge a fee for the bet. One common way of extracting an edge is to simply make it a bit tougher for the player to win. The benefit (to the casino) of this latter method is that payoffs can be a convenient 1:1 rather than an awkward 99:100, and players are left to wonder exactly how much of an edge the casino is getting.

One of the trickiest things that a casino will do is offer a big fat payoff, some-

Smarter Bet Tip
There's nothing wrong with occasionally risking a few dollars on an unfamiliar bet when you don't know the odds, but if you're planning to risk a substantial portion of your gambling bankroll, then it always pays to do some research and know the exact probability of winning.

thing enticing like 30:1. Unfortunately, the odds of winning are 35:1. It takes a calculator, a spreadsheet, or a book like this one to reveal the real probability of winning.

Five Dangerous Gambling Mistakes

While we're on the subject of odds (the rules of the universe), this is a good place to discuss the other universal rules that apply to any gambling game, especially craps. These are mistakes that will bust your bankroll faster than the worst house odds.

GOING "ON TILT"

It's easy to slip into a bad mood or be fatigued without realizing it, especially in the heat of a game. Pros use the term **on tilt** to describe a mood that adversely affects judgment. You should stop playing when you're tired. Stop when you're hungry. Stop when you're frustrated. Remember, games should be fun. If you're not having fun, go do something else. Continuing to play will only make the mood (and your potential losses) worse.

DRINKING ALCOHOL WHILE GAMBLING

Drinks are "free" in many casinos when playing at the tables and machines. Gee, aren't those casino guys nice? Toast them with a complimentary coffee or a soda, and stay away from the alcohol. Inebriating drinks cloud a player's judgment and inevitably earn the casino many times more than the value of the beverage.

Don't surrender that edge. Stick to strategy, win some money, and buy your drink later.

GOING OVER OR UNDER YOUR LIMITS

We'll talk about setting limits in a later chapter. The important thing to remember here is that limits are established in advance when your mind is clear precisely because casinos can be confusing. You will be constantly tempted to bet more, play more, or wager in ways that are unwise. Never give in to the temptation. Always follow your optimal stop-loss and win-limit strategies.

PLAYING FOR COMPS

Ten-dollar bets will get you free drinks and friendly service in a typical casino. Twenty-five dollar bets will usually result in a discounted room. One hundred dollar bets and above usually garner free meals and discounted or free rooms. By the time you're pushing around multiple black chips ($100 units), gregarious casino hosts in stylish suits will be treating you as a respected and dear friend. You'll be addressed warmly by your last initial, "Mr. P, it's great to see you again!" Yes, comps (complimentary rewards and incentives) are a nice perk if you were already planning to risk forty or fifty Ben Franklins, but increasing bets to get comps is financially foolish. The value of the comp is typically one-third or less of your expected loss. Don't get caught up in that ridiculous system of faux status. First establish betting levels and session lengths that suit your bankroll, and then negotiate comps at the casino.

TAKING THE GAME PERSONALLY

The purpose of the game is to generate excitement. Shout, cheer, cry if you must, but remember it's just a game. Revel in your winnings, lament your losses, but don't take either situation personally. Streaks happen. Luck will sometimes kiss you sweetly, and other nights it will slap you down with a vengeance. Remember, it's not about you.

Of course, there is one big exception to this last rule. If you play poorly and cost yourself money as a result, then you should take it personally! Luck is one thing; bad play is something entirely different. Learn from the mistake and resolve to never do that again.

In Review

🎲 **Positive-expectation games** are long-term money earners for the person (or entity) playing the positive side. The opposite side of the game has negative-expectation. Craps is a negative-expectation game for casino players.

🎲 **True odds** are a measure of probability. House odds are a measure of how much a casino will pay on your winning bet. The difference is the house edge, or profit for the casino. A larger edge means the casino has a greater advantage.

🎲 **Optimal strategy** can reduce and in some cases eliminate the house edge.

Chapter

Craps is About the Dice

IT'S IRONIC THAT THE CASINO GAME WITH THE LARGEST AND most complex table is really not at all about the table. You could play craps in a teacup. In fact, one of the reasons why craps (via its predecessor, hazard) has a history that stretches back nearly one thousand years is that it's such a physically convenient game to play. You can carry the dice in your pocket and play almost anywhere. As I mentioned in the introduction, that's what made craps so popular with soldiers. That's how it developed a Rat-Pack tough-guy image.

So, forget the table, or **layout**, for now. We'll use it later to help organize the bets. In this section, we'll talk about the dice.

How Will the Dice Roll?

A standard pair of dice can make thirty-six combinations that total eleven numbers (2 to 12). The table "Dice Combinations" (see page 28) shows the various possible sequences.

Let's say you're the craps **shooter** (the person throwing the dice). On your first roll, called the **come-out** roll, there are two numbers that can win and three that can lose. The winners are 7 and 11. If you roll 7 or 11, the contest is over. You rolled a **natural** and **passed**.

If you roll 2, 3, or 12, it's **craps**—you **don't pass**—you lose, and the contest is over.

Most of the time you won't roll a natural or craps; the come-out roll will be 4, 5, 6, 8, 9, or 10. When that happens the number becomes your **point**. You must roll the same number again to pass. There is no limit to the attempts allowed for a pass. You can pass in one roll or one hundred. After a point is established the only way to lose is to roll a 7. Yes, it was good for the come-out, but now it's bad. All the other numbers (including 11 and craps) have no importance at this stage. Roll the point and you win; roll 7 and you lose. End of contest; the next roll is a come-out.

That's it. That's basic craps. Very simple. A winning wager pays 1:1 (even money). The table on page 28 shows the various rolls required for a pass and the probabilities (true odds) for each outcome.

Of course, there is much more to craps than pass and don't pass, but it's mostly about the shooter and this contest. If you understand how to pass, you understand craps.

Dice Combinations

#	Ways to Roll	Combinations						True Odds	Percent Probability
2	1	1-1						35:1	2.8%
3	2	1-2	2-1					17:1	5.6%
4	3	2-2	1-3	3-1				11:1	8.3%
5	4	1-4	4-1	2-3	3-2			8:1	11.1%
6	5	3-3	2-4	4-2	1-5	5-1		6.2:1	13.9%
7	6	1-6	6-1	2-5	5-2	3-4	4-3	5:1	16.7%
8	5	4-4	2-6	6-2	5-3	3-5		6.2:1	13.9%
9	4	3-6	6-3	4-5	5-4			8:1	11.1%
10	3	5-5	4-6	6-4				11:1	8.3%
11	2	5-6	6-5					17:1	5.6%
12	1	6-6						35:1	2.8%

A pair of dice can create thirty-six possible combinations. Each cube has six sides and 6 x 6 = 36.

Percent probabilities in the far right column are rounded.

Wagers on pass have a house edge of 1.41%. In other words, the casino will earn an average of $14 for every $1,000 you wager. That's not too bad when you consider that they're supplying the table, the crew, and a palatial atmosphere. Just the smallest amount of luck can easily push you into the plus column.

Pass vs. Don't Pass

Strict regulations these days insure that craps games are honest, no loaded dice and no hanky-panky. But in the old days when you had to knock on a door and whisper a password to play craps, the integrity of the game wasn't always so absolute. What could you do if you didn't trust the dice? The obvious solution was to bet against the shooter. That option is still available to this day.

A wager on **don't pass** is essentially the reverse of betting on pass. Naturals (7 or 11) lose on the come-out. Craps wins (with one exception). Making the point loses. **Seven-out,** or rolling a 7 before a point, wins.

The one exception is 12 on the come-out. It's a **push,** or tie. No money changes hands. That small adjustment gives the house its entire advantage. If 12 wasn't a push, then you could earn 1.41% just like the casino. Pushing the 12 shifts the edge to the opposite side. The house advantage on the don't pass is 1.36% (from here forward we'll round these bets to the nearest tenth, 1.4%).

This yin-yang, do-don't concept is repeated throughout the game of craps. Most of the bets can be played on both sides. Some

Winning and Losing Rolls
for the Shooter

Come-out Roll	Numbers	Probability of Rolling
Pass (win) with natural	7,11	22.2%
Don't pass (lose) with craps	2,3,12	11.1%
Point	4,5,6,8,9,10	66.7%
Rolling to Repeat the Point		
Pass (win) with point	Point	8.3% to 13.9%
Don't pass (lose) with 7	7	16.7%
No effect	All other numbers	69.4% to 75%

A come-out roll is twice as likely to pass with a natural than lose with craps. The most likely outcome is establishing a point. If a point is established, the shooter must roll the point again to pass. 7 becomes a loser. Rolling 7 after the come-out is called a "seven-out."

people use the terms "right" or "wrong" when describing these wagers. Others say that "do" bettors are "against the house" and "don't bettors" are "with the house." Such phrases aren't quite accurate, and they're also a bit pejorative, but you will hear them from time to time. Just remember that the house always has an edge. It might be psychologically upsetting for some people to see other players betting "against" them, but it's really no worse than betting red when someone else bets black at roulette. The house handles both wagers.

Smarter Bet Tip
Some casinos "bar the 2" instead of the 12 on don't-pass wagers. Changing the push (tie) from 12 to 2 has no effect on the house edge or the overall probability of winning.

Playing the Basic Game

There are dozens of interesting craps bets that we'll cover in Chapters 3, 4 and 5, but right now let's talk about the practical aspects of playing the game.

Craps is played on a table like the one pictured on page 33. It's big, typically five by ten feet (1.5 x 3m). The sides are high to prevent dice from coming off the layout. The top edge has a rail with grooves to hold your chips, and below that is a ledge for drinks. It's everything necessary to shoot craps like a member of the Rat Pack.

Notice that the layout has boxes that correspond to the various points, and a long strip called the **pass line** that runs nearly the length of the table. Above that is an area labeled "don't pass."

The dealer at the center of the table holding the long curved stick is the **stickperson** (the older term "stickman" persists in many venues). She retrieves dice after a throw, returns them to the shooter, and is responsible for all other issues concerning the cubes.

Across from the stickperson is the **boxperson** (often referred to as "boxman"). He keeps an eye on the bank of casino chips and supervises the game. Most disputes are settled by his decision. On either side of the boxperson are dealers who pay bets, take wagers, position bets for players, and generally run the game.

BUYING IN

Buying into craps is a little different from some other games because the table may be busy and you may have to get the dealer's attention. Put your money on the layout (when the dice aren't rolling) and say "change" in a clear voice. Don't attempt to hand anything to the dealer. Security procedures require that money and chips be displayed on the table before being converted. The bills will be counted, and a dealer will give you chips in whatever denomination you request.

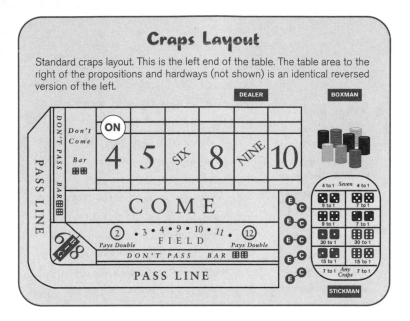

Craps Layout

Standard craps layout. This is the left end of the table. The table area to the right of the propositions and hardways (not shown) is an identical reversed version of the left.

BETTING

For obvious reasons, pass and don't-pass wagers are made only when a shooter is coming out (there's an oddball exception to this rule in Chapter 4, but for now let's stick to the typical wagers). You'll know when a shooter is coming out by finding the **puck**. It's a large disk that's black on one side and white on the other. "ON" or "POINT" is printed on the white side; "OFF" or "COME-OUT" is printed on the black side.

The puck will be in or near the section of the layout marked **don't come** with the OFF side up when the shooter is coming out.

It will be moved to a corresponding number box and turned to the ON side after a point has been established. When the puck is OFF, just lay your wager on the pass line or the **don't-pass bar**.

A dealer will double your chips or take them away depending on the results of the rolls. Be sure to remove your winnings from the layout in a timely fashion. Too many high-fives and cheers may cause you to miss the next roll, and the rule is "if it lays, it plays." Your money could be gone before the celebration has concluded.

THROWING THE DICE

Shooting isn't mandatory, but it's a lot of fun.

When the stickperson offers you dice, either choose two from the selection or decline. If you decline, the person next to you will be offered the dice. If you decide to throw, you'll hear the stickperson say, "Shooter coming out!"

Throw the dice hard enough to hit the wall at the other end of the table. This is very important. A throw in which the

Puck Positions

OFF or COME-OUT = Shooter is coming out

ON or POINT = Shooter is trying to roll a point

dice don't take a bounce at the end may be considered a **no roll**. This will make you very unpopular with the crew and the other players, especially if the invalid numbers would have paid someone big money.

Time-consuming rituals before throwing are equally unloved. It's okay to rattle the dice for a few moments or whisper a mantra, but elaborate performances are not appreciated. Keep your throwing hand in sight at all times when holding the cubes. Don't hold or touch them with both hands. Don't smack the cubes on the surface of the table. Don't grind or rub the cubes together. Why all the rules? You'd be amazed at the sneaky things people do to cheat. The craps crew has seen it all, so they're extra cautious when a player

Smarter Bet Tip
Some people believe that setting dice (positioning them in a particular way before a throw) can improve the chances of a pass. See Chapter 6 for more on this strategy.

Always throw dice hard enough to hit the end of the table, but don't throw them so wildly that they come off the table. The game will be delayed until the dice are found and checked for tampering. Some superstitious shooters request "same dice" if the cubes escape because they believe changing dice will cause a seven-out.

handles dice in an irregular way. It's best to simply take the cubes and throw them.

You're allowed to shoot indefinitely, as long as you continue to pass with a natural on the come-out, roll craps, pass with a point, or roll numbers other than 7 after a come-out. If you seven-out, it's over. You lose and the dice are offered to the person standing next to you.

Everyone gets a chance to shoot, but players betting the don't pass often decline the dice. If they do take the dice, the stickperson will announce that the player is shooting from the don't. Other players may refuse to bet until the dice have passed. There is no practical or mathematical reason for any of this. It's just custom and superstition (see Chapter 8) but remember that craps is a social game. If you're playing alone, or it's just you and friends, then it really doesn't matter. On the other hand, shooting from the don't is a judgment call when the table is crammed with strangers. Are you feeling like a maverick? Then go ahead, shoot from the don't.

In Review

⚄ **The shooter's attempt to pass** is the basic contest in craps. Players can wager with the shooter on the pass line or against the shooter on the don't-pass bar. These do and don't bets have a house edge of 1.4%.

⚄ **You can tell if a shooter is coming out** or throwing for a point by finding the puck on the layout. It will show "OFF" or "COME-OUT" when the shooter is starting a new pass, and "ON" or "POINT" when the shooter is trying to throw a point.

⚄ **The craps crew consists of** a stickperson who controls the dice, a boxperson who supervises the game, and dealers who handle the bets.

⚄ **You should throw the dice with one hand,** and be sure they take a bounce off the wall at the far end of the table. But don't throw them so hard that they fly off the table. That will delay the game.

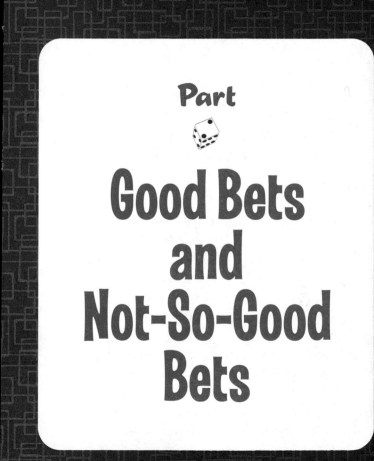

Part

Good Bets and Not-So-Good Bets

Chapter

The Best Craps Bets

THE AVERAGE PASS ATTEMPT takes about four or five rolls, though **boomerang** rolls (point-point) are quite common, as are point followed by an immediate seven-out. Naturals and craps on the come-out are also pretty frequent. But even though there are plenty of quick decisions that can occur for pass and don't pass, the reverse is also true. It can take twenty minutes or longer for a shooter to hit her point or seven-out. Craps lore is filled with amazing stories of people who have held the dice for an hour or more. A feat like that would be extraordinarily boring if the only wagers at stake were the pass and don't pass. But craps is an exciting game because every roll can be a winner. Imagine an hour of non-stop luck! Even twenty minutes with the dice can be a golden eternity.

The extra action comes from the bets we cover in this chapter and the next two.

Pass and Don't Pass: A Second Look

I mentioned this previously, but it bears repeating: pass and don't pass have a 1.4% house edge, making them extremely good craps bets. They also compare favorably to most other casino wagers. Slots are generally four to six times less advantageous! Roulette on an American wheel is nearly four times more expensive, as is Caribbean Stud Poker. Baccarat is roughly comparable to craps; blackjack is just a bit better.

The popular media image of craps as a game that quickly consumes money comes from the bad reputation of bets that we'll review later. Pass and don't pass are pussycats in comparison. They're the basic components for all of the wagers in this chapter.

Smarter Bet Factoid
Shooters are usually required to make a line bet (a bet on the pass or don't pass). This ensures that they have a stake in the way the dice are rolled.

Come and Don't Come

Come is the largest area of the layout on most tables. It's the first thing most people see (or at least the first thing that registers) when they peer over the rail. What the heck does it mean?

The origin of the phrase is lost in the mists of time, but you'll find it helpful to consider come as a hearty welcome to players who have arrived at the game during the shooter's attempt to pass.

It's simple. A come bet works like a pass-line bet except that a come bet is made after the shooter establishes a point. Nevertheless, the wager has a full opportunity for a natural win on the first roll.

How does that work? The key to understanding come (and its opposite, **don't come**) is to forget about the shooter's attempt to pass and simply focus on the numbers as the shooter rolls them. Think of the numbers as a series. Remember, the rules for winning and losing are exactly the same for pass and for come.

For example, a come wager will win on the first roll when the dice produce 7 or 11, and it will lose with craps. A winning 7 for a come bet might be a seven-out for the shooter, but the shooter's contest doesn't involve the come bet. A come bet has its own come-out and its own point. Come is entirely independent of the shooter's attempt to pass except that both wagers use the same sequence of numbers.

The table opposite shows how this works. Imagine that four players simultaneously arrive at the table. Each player bets only one way and waits for a win or loss before placing another

Do and Don't Betting Examples

Roll	Dice Results	Pass	Don't Pass	Come	Don't Come
1	7	win come out	lose come out	no action	no action
2	6	point est.	point est.	no action	no action
3	3			lose craps	win craps
4	4			point est.	point est.
5	12				
6	5				
7	10				
8	4			win point	lose point
9	2			lose craps	win craps
10	3			lose craps	win craps
11	2			lose craps	win craps
12	6	win point	lose point	point est.	point est.
13	8	point est.	point est.		
14	6			win point	lose point
15	7	lose (7 out)	win (7 out)	win come-out	lose come-out
16	11	win come out	lose come out	no action	no action
17	5	point est.	point est.	no action	no action
18	9			point est.	point est.
19	7	lose (7 out)	win (7 out)	lose (7 out)	win (7 out)
Total		**3 wins 2 losses**	**2 wins 3 losses**	**3 wins 5 losses**	**5 wins 3 losses**

Pass and don't-pass bets are made when the shooter is coming out. Come and don't-come bets are made after a shooter's point has been established. Wins and losses in this table reflect these particular random dice rolls.

bet. The various wagers are shown side by side. They all occur during the same random rolls of the dice. Empty spaces indicate no effect from the roll.

Notice that the first roll in the sequence is the shooter's come-out. It has no effect on the come and don't come because action is not allowed for those wagers. The second 7 (fifteenth roll in the sequence) is a win for the come but a loss for the shooter. The third 7 (final roll in the sequence) is a loss for both do bettors and a win for both don't bettors.

There is no limit to the number of come and don't-come wagers a player can make alone or in tandem with other bets. Betting on multiple successive rolls is common, though it can get expensive. If a shooter throws 7, the current come bet will win, but the others that are waiting for a point will be lost. On the other hand, if the shooter is throwing a lot of numbers and 7 is nowhere to be seen, multiple come bets will earn a lot of money. And of course, the opposite is true for multiple don't-come bets; one 7 brings rich rewards, but a hot shooter will knock off multiple don't-come bets like a kung fu master in a martial arts movie.

Pass Line vs. Come: Practical Differences

A bet on come has the exact same house edge (1.4%) and overall probability of winning or losing as a bet on the pass line. Ditto for don't come and don't pass. But there are some practical differences beyond the issue of when the bets are allowed.

Come and don't come belong to a category of craps wagers that are handled in whole or in part by a dealer. Points are not recorded with a puck. Instead, the chips are moved into the numbered squares, an area that is off-limits to the players. Here's how it works for come.

As with line wagers, you begin by noting whether the shooter is coming out or trying to roll a point. You can make a come bet if the puck is ON.

Just reach across the layout and put your chips on the come. Come bets that win or lose on the first roll are handled like any bet; they're either paid or taken. If a point is rolled, a dealer moves the come bet to the corresponding number box on the layout. The exact placement of the chips in the box will reflect where you're standing at the table. The chips will stay there until a 7 or the point is rolled. A 7 makes them disappear, but a point will bring them back to the come box with a matching pile of chips—your winnings.

If you're making multiple come bets of equal value and a previous one happens to win while the current one has just established a point, the dealer won't bother switching equal stacks of chips. He will just pay the bet. This is called **off and on**, and it's one of the many informal customs that make craps so charming.

Wagers on the don't come are placed and handled similarly to come bets. Simply put your chips on the don't come. They're moved to a corresponding number box if a point is rolled. A 7 brings the wager back with matching funds; a point makes it disappear.

Odds: The Best Bet in the House

Craps is a wonderfully quirky game, especially the terminology. Phrases like "bet the don't come" and "win the don't pass" severely stretch the capabilities of the English language. The term "odds" is the ultimate example of craps' jabberwocky. I'm not talking about true odds or house odds. Craps has a bet called "odds." Yes, it's strange, but it's worth the linguistic confusion because an odds wager has a zero percent house edge! When you are betting odds, house odds are identical to true odds.

Got that?

Odds is the best bet available on a craps table, and it's frequently the best bet you can get in a casino. Odds is even better than playing blackjack (unless you're counting cards).

Here's how it works. Odds is technically a standalone bet, a separate wager, but it is always linked to an original **flat bet** on pass or come, don't pass or don't come. Odds for a do bet is called **taking**

Examples of Taking and Laying Odds

Point	True Odds	Taking Odds (Do) $30 Bet Returns	Laying Odds (Don't) $30 Bet Returns
4	2:1	$60	$15
5	3:2	$45	$20
6	6:5	$36	$25
8	6:5	$36	$25
9	3:2	$45	$20
10	2:1	$60	$15

True odds are against the point. For example, odds are 2:1 against rolling 4 before 7. That's because there are six ways to roll a 7 and only three ways to roll a 4. Odds bets are paid at true odds and have no house edge

odds; it's an extra wager (made after the come-out) that the shooter will successfully roll the point. **Laying odds** is the opposite of taking odds. It's a bet that is hoping for a seven-out. The table above shows the various payoffs.

Odds don't earn the casino any money; they're a premium. So the house has a lot of rules restricting the wagers (sort of like fine print on a discount coupon).

Do vs. Don't Odds Comparison

	Base Bet	3X Odds Bet (point is 10)	Bet Total	Win Total	Win Probability (against)
DO	$10	$30 (3 x $10 base bet)	$40	$70	2:1
DON'T	$10	$60 (3 x $20 bet payoff)	$70	$40	1:2

Win probability is true odds against the bet.

The first and most important rule is that odds are only allowed in multiples of the original flat bet, and there is always a limit. For example, if the flat bet is $10 and the odds allowed are 3X, you can take odds in any amount up to $30, and you can lay odds up to a $30 payoff.

Let's say the point is 10; a do wager is competing with a don't wager, and both players have 3X odds. The probability of making the point is 2:1 against because there are six ways to roll 7 and only three ways to roll 10. That's why laying odds (winning with a seven-out) doesn't pay as much as taking odds (winning with a point).

The table above shows the various amounts and possible payoffs for a flat bet and odds when the point is ten.

Keep in mind that the base bet is paid 1:1, and the odds bet is always paid at the true odds of winning. Also, odds must be taken or laid on the same side as the flat bet.

How much in odds can you take or lay at your favorite casino? The limits are posted along with the other table limits on a plastic card attached to the inside wall of the craps table. 3X for points 4/10, 4X for points 5/9, and 5X for points 6/8 is pretty standard these days, though 10X for all the points can be found at some properties. Occasionally you'll find a house that offers 100X, and casinos with a monopoly on the market often allow only 1X or 2X for all the points.

The Odd and Sneaky Side of Odds

The tricky thing about odds is that there is no place for the bet on the layout. It's a bit like an "off the menu" special; odds is available only to people who know enough to ask.

Taking odds on the pass line is easy. Put your chips directly behind the original bet (on the blank space next to the wall) after the point is made. Your bet will be paid or swept away as the dice warrant.

Laying odds on the don't pass is a little weird. You place the chips next to the original bet, but you **heel** the stack. That means the bottom chip is off center and the stack slants to one side. The dealer will show you how to do it. Odds bets are heeled when the payoff will be a different amount than the payoff for the flat bet.

If the payoff will be the same then the stack should be **bridged** instead of heeled. A bridged stack is two stacks with a third perched on top. Again, the dealer will show you how it's done.

Yes, it's arcane, but for a house edge of zero percent the hassle is worth it.

Taking and laying odds on the come and don't come require a dealer's assistance. You do this by putting chips on the layout (preferably on a line that separates betting spaces). Tell the dealer that you want "odds on the four" or "odds on the nine." She will pick up the chips and place the wager accordingly.

One of the most important things to remember about taking odds is to do it in multiples that the casino can pay. If the point is 6 and you take $8 odds, the payoff would be $9.60. The casino will only give you $9. To get the full payout you must take odds in multiples of $5 when the point is 6 or 8, $2 for points 5 and 9. And any whole-dollar amount is fine for points 4 and 10.

Do it in reverse when laying odds. Odds on 4/10 should be divisible by two, 5/9 by three, and 6/8 by six.

Working Bets and Taking Wagers Down

Most casino games **trap** a bet once it's made. The reels spin or the cards snap and a decision is rendered. Win, lose, or push, the contest is over. Craps is different because in most cases it doesn't trap a bet. Many rolls can occur before the dice deliver a decision. A **live** bet in this situation is said to be **working**. This is an important distinction because many craps bets can be turned on, turned off, or taken down (removed entirely) as a player wishes.

Odds is an excellent example of this. Let's say a shooter is giving you a bad feeling. You can temporarily turn off your come or don't-come odds, or even have the bet removed from the layout. It's perfectly okay. Just tell the dealer to "take the odds down." What happens if your best buddy gets the dice? Put your odds back up. The dealer will be happy to oblige. Pass and don't-pass are even easier: just reach over and remove the odds bet.

Unfortunately, basic pass or come wagers cannot be turned off or taken down. Remember, they have their best chance of winning (2:1) on the first roll, but they're at a big disadvantage after that. The casino takes the upfront risk, so it wants a shot at the reward. Those bets are trapped on the layout until a point or seven-out.

The reverse is true for don't-pass and don't-come wagers. It is you who takes

Smarter Bet Tip

One way to avoid misunderstandings when making bets that require dealer assistance is to put wagers on a line that separates betting areas. That way your odds on the ten won't accidentally become a brand new come bet.

the early risk, and it's you who has the distinct advantage after a point is rolled (between 2:1 and 6:5). So, you can remove or reduce a don't bet at any time. In fact, you'd be doing the casino a huge favor. But you can't put the bet back up once it's been taken down.

Here's another example of working bets. Most "do" players who are betting the pass line and come want come odds off during a come-out because a 7 is good for the pass but bad for the working come. Retrieving the odds wagers and replacing them on the next roll would be time consuming, so the casino shortens the process by considering come odds automatically off during a come-out unless you request otherwise. If you don't care about what happens on the pass line, tell the dealer you want odds to stay on.

In contrast, don't-come odds are not automatically off when the shooter is coming out because don't-come bettors are rooting with the pass line (only on that roll) and hoping for a 7.

In Review

⚅ **Pass and don't pass** have a low house edge (1.4%), and these two wagers form the basis for all of craps' best bets.

⚅ **Come and don't-come bets** are made after a point has been established. They are independent of the shooter's contest, but otherwise they operate by the same rules as pass and don't-pass. Come and don't-come have a 1.4% house edge.

⚅ **Odds is an additional bet** made in conjunction with a pass, don't pass, come or don't come wager. Odds wagers have a 0% house edge; this makes them the best bet in craps.

⚅ **Come, don't-come, and their related odds bets** are handled by dealers. The chips are moved into the numbered squares on the table to signify the working point. This part of the table is off-limits to the players.

⚅ **Odds bets can be turned on, off, or taken down** as the player prefers. Don't bets can be reduced or removed from the layout at any time. Do bets (pass and come) are trapped on the layout once a point is rolled.

⚅ **Odds on the come** are automatically off when a shooter is coming out.

Chapter

Playing the Numbers

IT'S AMAZING, but pass, don't pass, come, don't come, and odds (sometimes referred to as "free odds") make up just a fraction of the bets available on a craps table. There are more than two dozen others!

None of them are as good as the wagers we've previously covered. You wouldn't miss any bargains if you skipped this chapter and the next, but you would miss learning about some of the sneaky and amazing ways that a casino extracts a monster edge. Knowledge will also eliminate temptation, so you should read the next two chapters to avoid being lured by whiz-bang payoffs and bets that are oh-so convenient to make.

This chapter covers bets that are variations of taking or laying odds. Unfortunately, they're not "free."

Place Bets

Let's say a shooter throws the following sequence: 6,5,8,10,4,7. That's death to a do bettor; it's a bunch of points and then seven-out, a real drag. One alternative is to bet the don't, but there's no guarantee that the next sequence won't be 6,5,8,8,6,5. Another choice is to bet the numbers so they'll pay off the first time rather than just establish a point.

A **place bet** is simply a wager that a number will appear before 7. The table on page 56 shows the various place bets, the odds, and how they pay.

Notice that the 6 and 8 have an edge that's just 0.1% worse than a bet on the line or come, but the edge nearly triples or quadruples on the rest of the numbers. 4/10 pays $108, but free odds would return $120. A bettor may not notice the $12 difference if the dice produce a lot of points, but in the long run the winning won't keep pace with the losing. A roll of 7 will appear frequently enough to wipe out the profits. When would that happen? It might take hours, days, years, or it could happen on the next roll. We'll cover probability in Chapter 7, but for now just remember that the house edge works. That's how casinos pay for the plush carpets and chandeliers.

A place bet is handled in a similar way to odds. Just put money down and say "twelve on the eight" or "place it on the five." A dealer will move the chips to the appropriate box. Also note that 6 and 8 should be wagered in multiples of six. If you bet $25 you'll only be paid for a win on $24.

Place Bets

Number	True Odds (against)	House Odds	$60 Bet Pays	Place House Edge
4	2:1	9:5	$108	6.7%
5	3:2	7:5	$84	4.0%
6	6:5	7:6	$70	1.5%
8	6:5	7:6	$70	1.5%
9	3:2	7:5	$84	4.0%
10	2:1	9:5	$108	6.7%

Place bets are automatically off during a come-out. And of course, you can take them down at any time.

Buy Bets

Buy bets are similar to place bets, but they're paid at true odds. Sounds great! Did I mention the vig? What's a vig? It's short for **vigorish**, and it's basically a fee or percent charge for making a bet. Strictly speaking, vigorish is synonymous with any casino house edge. Slots, blackjack, and all the other games have vigorish, but the word is mostly used in situations that involve a betting fee.

Buy bets have a vig of 5% on the wager. Otherwise, they're handled like place bets. Tell the dealer which number you want to buy, and he'll take the vig and then move the chips to the appropriate box.

The vig is returned if the bet is taken down. An additional vig is charged every time the dice deliver a decision. Some casinos only charge a vig on winning wagers and that drops the edge considerably, particularly on the outside numbers (4/10).

As with place bets, buy bets are automatically off during a come-out, and you can take them down at any time.

Lay Bets

Lay bets (sometimes called no bets) are the mirror opposite of buy bets. They pay true odds when the shooter rolls a 7 before the number. That makes a lay bet essentially the same as laying odds except a 5% vig is charged on the amount to be won.

As with buy bets, the vig is returned if the bet is taken down. An additional vig is charged every time the dice produce a

Smarter Bet Factoid
A put bet is a pass-line or come wager that is made or increased after a point has been established. In other words, no come-out. Why would anyone do that? It's a thoroughly rotten bet unless the player takes odds. A put bet with 10X odds has a lower house edge than a buy or place bet.

Buy Bets

Number	True Odds (against)	$60 Bet Pays	5% Vig	Buy House Edge (standard)	Buy House Edge (vig on win only)
4	2:1	$120	3	4.8%	1.6%
5	3:2	$90	3	4.8%	1.9%
6	6:5	$72	3	4.8%	2.2%
8	6:5	$72	3	4.8%	2.2%
9	3:2	$90	3	4.8%	1.9%
10	2:1	$120	3	4.8%	1.6%

Note that the total bet is actually $63 even though the payoff is based on $60.

Lay Bets

Number	True Odds (against)	$120 Bet Pays	5% Vig	Lay House Edge (standard)	Buy House Edge (vig on win only)
4	1:2	$60	3	2.4%	1.6%
5	2:3	$80	4	3.2%	1.9%
6	5:6	$100	5	4.0%	2.2%
8	5:6	$100	5	4.0%	2.2%
9	2:3	$80	4	3.2%	1.9%
10	1:2	$60	3	2.4%	1.6%

Note that the total bet is actually $120 plus the vig even though the payoff is based on $120.

decision. Also note that some casinos charge a vig only on winning wagers.

Lay bets are always on unless you request them to be turned off.

Squeezing the House

Some players squeeze a little extra value from their buy and lay bets when they wager an amount that cannot be conveniently charged in whole dollars equal to five percent. Casinos typically round down on vig amounts less than fifty cents and round up otherwise, so a $25 buy bet (one green chip) would be charged only $1. That drops the house edge by about one percent. The exact amount depends on how much you squeeze.

Of course, if a player really wants to squeeze the house, then the best strategy is to avoid place, buy, and lay bets altogether. Some craps enthusiasts would argue that they're not "bad" bets when compared to slots, roulette, and Caribbean Stud Poker. That's true, but they're less than ideal. The world won't end if you play them. Just be aware that you'll be paying for the pleasure.

Smarter Bet Tip
Most casinos charge a minimum $1 vig for buy and lay bets, so a bet for any amount less than $20 effectively increases the 5% vig.

In Review

✦ **Place bets and buy bets** are similar to taking odds, but they don't require a previous wager on the line or come. Unfortunately, the house pays less than true odds for winning place bets and charges a 5% vig (fee) for buy bets.

✦ **Lay bets are similar to laying odds on the don't**, but a bet on the bar or don't come is not required. The house charges a 5% vig on the amount to be won.

✦ **Casinos charge the vig** in whole dollar amounts, so players effectively get a discount if they wager in units that cause the casino to round the vig down.

Chapter

From Bad to Worse

THESE ARE THE SUCKER BETS that your mother warned you not to make. These are the legendary wagers that have broken millionaires and laid waste to fat bankrolls. Much of craps' bad reputation rests on these extremely disadvantageous gambles.

The one thing that most of them have in common is that they pay handsomely when luck is your lover. But when luck leads you with teasing kisses and sweet promises into a dark corner and then mugs you, it's usually these bets that come crashing down on your head. You should avoid them all without exception, but in the interest of being comprehensive, we'll review them here.

Playing the Field and Other Rotten Bets

Just below the area for come and above the don't pass is a section on the layout known as the **field**. A bet here can be made at any time without dealer assistance. It's an even-money wager that the next roll of the dice will be 3, 4, 9, 10, or 11; if the dice roll 2 or 12, the casino pays double the wager (some casinos pay triple). 5, 6, 7 and 8 are losers. Eight winning numbers and only four losers may seem like a good bet but the true odds are 20:16 against the field. The house edge on a field bet is 5.6% when 2 and 12 pay double. It drops to 2.8% if 2 and 12 pay triple. That's worse than roulette, though it's still better than most slot games. Of course, a slot machine might give you a jackpot. The best you'll do on the field is 3:1.

People who play the field do it because it allows them to simultaneously cover many numbers without putting up a lot of money. One bet covers forty-four percent of all the number combinations, including craps and 11. That means the dealer is frequently pushing chips to players who bet the field. Unfortunately, he takes chips away at an even greater frequency.

BIG SIX AND BIG EIGHT

Big six and **big eight** are found in the corners of some layouts, and they are the ultimate sucker bets. Each is a wager on one number, either 6 or 8, to roll before the 7. Big six or big eight works exactly like a place bet except the payoff is even money.

That's right. $30 on the big six wins $30. The same money "place the six" will bring $35.

Why would anyone play the big six/eight? It's usually a favorite of minimum-bet players who don't want to put up the few extra dollars it takes to properly place the numbers. Others bet big six/eight out of ignorance or because they don't like to work with dealers (the bets can be made without dealer assistance).

The house edge on big six/eight is a nasty 9.1%. That's comparable to a progressive slot machine, but without the one-in-a-few million chance of winning a fortune. Big six/eight simply bleeds its suckers dry. The bet is so bad that it's not allowed in Atlantic City.

HARDWAYS

A 4, 6, 8, or 10 thrown as a double is called a **hard number** because it is produced the hard way. Betting the **hardway** is a wager that a particular number will be thrown hard before a 7, and before it is thrown the easy way. Hard four and hard ten pay 7:1. Hard six and hard eight pay 9:1. The area for these bets is at the center of the table, and they're sometimes called all-day bets because they can stay out there for quite a while if the shooter doesn't throw the number or 7. The bet can be made at any time and withdrawn at any time; it requires dealer assistance. Just put your chips on the table and tell the dealer what you want…if you dare. The house edge for 6 and 8 is a painful 9.1%. It's an excruciating 11.1% for 4 and 10.

Craps' Worst Bets

Bet	True Odds	House Odds	House Edge
Any seven (big red)	5:1	4:1	16.7%
Two (snake eyes)	35:1	30:1	13.9%
Twelve (boxcars)	35:1	30:1	13.9%
Hop (1 way)	35:1	30:1	13.9%
Whirl	10:5	8:5	13.3%
Horn	20:4	17:4	12.5%
Hop (2 ways)	17:1	15:1	11.1%
Three (ace-deuce)	17:1	15:1	11.1%
Eleven (yo-leven)	17:1	15:1	11.1%
Any craps	8:1	7:1	11.1%
Hard four	8:1	7:1	11.1%
Hard ten	8:1	7:1	11.1%
Hard six	10:1	9:1	9.1%
Hard eight	10:1	9:1	9.1%
Big six/eight	6.5	1:1	9.1%

Odds and payoffs for horn and whirl are an average (individual wins pay differently).

The Rest of the Worst

The rest of the bets in the center of the table aren't better than the hardways, and they're frequently worse.

They're all one-roll **propositions**, and they're handled by the stickperson. The table on page 65 shows the various bets, true odds, house odds, and the house edge. It's a real rogues' gallery.

This is where the craps jargon really explodes. For example, **horn** is a combined bet on 2, 3, 11, and 12. The payoff is calculated as if you had bet each number separately. Your wager is divided into quarters, so if you make this long-shot bet it's a good idea to put money down in multiples of four or request a **horn high** and indicate on which of the four you want the extra money: "Horn high 12!"

Whirl is a horn bet with the 7 added. The bet is divided into five parts. **C&E** is craps plus 11. **Buffalo** is a combination of the four hardways plus a 7 or sometimes a "yo" 11. **Boxcars** is a bet on 12. A **hop bet** is a wager that a single number will be thrown in a particular way on the very next roll. Technically, 2, 3, 11, and 12 are hop bets, but you can do it with any number (assuming that you'd be willing to make such a bad wager).

It's a cornucopia of colorful names and slang for basically rotten gambling. There isn't a single bet in the center of the table that has a house edge of less than 9%. Betting the seven (big red) is a whopping 16.7%. That's the worst bet available in many casinos.

In Review

🎲 **The field is a one-roll bet that pays 1:1** when the dice produce 3, 4, 9, 10, or 11; it pays double (or in some casinos triple) for 2 and 12. Nevertheless, the field is not a good wager. It has a house edge of 5.6%

🎲 **Big six and big eight are sucker bets.** They have an edge of 9.1%

🎲 **Hardways and propositions** (one-roll bets) are all extremely poor wagers with house edges that range from 9.1% to 16.7%.

Part

Advanced Strategies

Chapter

Reducing the House Edge

HERE'S SOMETHING WE ALL LEARNED AS CHILDREN. IT'S a principle that applies directly to the topics in the next few chapters.

$$1 + 2 = 3$$

And, of course, switching the order of the numbers doesn't change the sum.

$$2 + 1 = 3$$

No matter how we divide or merge three units, the result will always be three, and never four.

$$1 + 1 + 1 = 3$$

Yes, it's simple enough, but craps' cornucopia of betting options tends to obscure this basic truth:

A combination of bets will never outperform the combination's individual components.

Never ever. And yet some people can't resist the challenge of trying to pull four out of three.

Trimming the Hedges

Hedge bets are tricky systems that involve combining bets to supposedly reduce risk. They actually do work to the extent that they protect against one particular result, but the alternative is usually even more expensive. For example, some bettors "insure" the pass line by also betting any craps. That supposedly turns the first roll into a can't-lose bet. Right? Wrong! Let's do the arithmetic. The table titled "Craps Insurance" (see page 72) shows why insuring the pass line is a mistake.

In this example $20 is wagered on the pass line and $5 is wagered on any craps.

Smarter Bet Tip
The first step to reducing the craps house edge is to avoid anything that increases it. That includes all bets in the center of the table. There is no system or wagering combination that can improve propositions and hardways even when they are used as "insurance."

Craps Insurance

	Ways To Win	Ways To Lose	No Effect (point)	Total Average Dollars Won
Line Bet $20	8	4	24	$80
Line Bet $20 and Any Craps $5	12	24	0	$60

The above numbers represent average results after thirty-six come-out rolls.

Seven-Out Insurance

	Point	Ways To Win	Ways To Lose	No Effect	Total Average Dollars Lost
Line bet $20	6/8	5	6	25	-$20
Line bet $20 and any seven $10	6/8	11	25	0	-$80

The above numbers represent average results after thirty-six rolls.

The combination guarantees that the first roll will always win $15 or establish a point at a cost of $5. Unfortunately those points come frequently enough to wipe out the advantage of winning on craps. The line bet does much better by itself.

Keep in mind that a bet on the pass-line has its greatest probability of winning on the come out. The above system hedges the bet precisely when it needs it the least.

Okay, so how about betting any seven (often referred to as **big red**) once a point has been made? That would avoid a loss on seven-out, right? Yes, but only if a 7 or the point appears immediately. Those pesky dice are generally not so cooperative. The true odds against seven are 5:1, and it may take a dozen or more rolls before big red finally makes an appearance. Meanwhile, every other number is a loser.

The table opposite shows that big red costs much more than it earns (on average) after thirty-six rolls. In this example it quadruples the expense of rolling 6/8. Betting any seven with 5/9 or 4/10 is even worse.

That realization causes hedge bettors to search for new ways to protect their money against loss. Betting the field? Betting the hardways? Buying the numbers? It can't be done. The smart way to bet craps is to pick a wager with a low house edge and make it even lower.

Flat Bets Combined with Odds

Pass Line/Come	1.41%
With 1x odds	0.85%
With 2x odds	0.61%
With 3x odds	0.47%
With 5x odds	0.33%
With 10x odds	0.19%
With 20x odds	0.10%
With 100x odds	0.02%
Don't Pass/Don't Come	1.36%
With 1x odds	0.69%
With 2x odds	0.46%
With 3x odds	0.34%
With 5x odds	0.23%
With 10x odds	0.12%
With 20x odds	0.07%
With 100x odds	0.01%

The house edge on odds is always 0%. The figures in the right column show the overall house edge when odds are combined with a flat bet.

Flat Bets with Odds

Pass, don't pass, come, and don't come have a house edge of 1.4%. That's pretty low, but the table on the opposite page shows happens when odds are added to the equation.

Remember, the actual house edge on the flat bet doesn't change. $120 on the pass line will always be subject to a 1.4% house edge regardless of the odds allowed. But what if you didn't put $120 on the pass line? If you wager $60 on the line and take $60 in odds (1x), then the average house edge on the combined bet drops to 0.85%. $20 on the line and $100 in odds (5x) will bring the house edge down to 0.33%.

Putting less on the line and more in odds always lowers the overall house edge. Of course, luck is luck. Don't confuse a lower house edge with an altered probability of any number appearing on the dice. 7 is always the favorite, and the true odds are always against making the point.

Effects of Betting
With and Without Odds

Dice Roll	Natural	Craps	Pass 4/10	Seven-Out
Probability	22.2%	11.1%	8.3%	16.6%
Pass $40 Wager Odds $0	+40	-40	+40	-40
Pass $10 Wager Odds $30 (3X)	+10	-10	+70	-40
Don't Pass $40 Wager Odds $0	-40	+40	-40	+40
Don't Pass $10 Wager Odds $60 (3X)	-10	+10	-70	+40

Natural and craps percentages reflect the come-out roll. Pass and seven-out percentages are for every roll after the point has been established. Points 4 and 10 are used in this example. Other points would produce different amounts. Remember that don't bets have an advantage after the come-out.

This leads to interesting objections from some players because odds is a separate wager. Reducing the amount on the line or come causes them to win less money if the dice tumble their way on the come-out.

It's a valid observation. The biggest opportunity for pass/come is on the come-out. Having less money on the line means less of a win if a natural appears. On the other hand, would you rather get 1:1 on a flat bet with a 1.4% disadvantage, or 6:5, 3:2, or 2:1 on a bet at true odds?

Just Say Whoa!

Casinos limit odds for a good reason. The bet has no profit margin, and dice can be unpredictable. A player taking odds can catch a long string of points and soak the house for major bucks. Yes, a point is the underdog, but it's spooky how 7 can sometimes disappear for an extended roll. That's ruinous if you're laying odds on the don't, especially because you lay more to win less.

So be careful about laying odds. There's a strong temptation to bet more than you might normally (especially on the 4/10) because the chance of winning is so high and the payoff is so low. But you should resist the temptation unless your bankroll and temperament can handle a large loss (and a table full of people cheering your worse-than-average bad luck).

Some players avoid this situation altogether by never laying odds. They simply load the don't and pray that a natural won't appear. Take another look at the chart on page 76. The biggest return on the don't is when you bet it all at the beginning rather than laying odds, but that's also the biggest risk. Laying odds is the mathematically superior option, but in this case the question I posed at the end of the last section is reversed. Would you rather get 1:1 on a flat bet with a 1.4% disadvantage, or 5:6, 2:3, or 1:2 on a bet at true odds?

It's a personal choice; just realize that you'll be taking an extra 1.4% risk if you skip odds and put it all onto the don't.

On the other hand, most casinos don't rate odds for comps the same way they rate flat bets, so shifting to odds may lower your comp rating. You should never increase bets for comps, but here it's an issue of changing bets. It's pointless to gain 1.4% if you lose 2% or more (of the value of your total action) in comps.

Placing the Six and Eight

Place six and place eight have a house edge of 1.5%, just a smidgen more than a line wager and still a pretty good bet. Players who bet don't pass and don't come sometimes place the six and eight as a short-term hedge. It's not a bad bet, but it does tend to reduce the return on the don't. It's also a gut call because you're predicting the shooter won't throw 7 in the next two or three rolls.

The best way to make this hedge bet is to be sure the combined total of the six and eight is not greater than the don't wager. Let's say $30 is on the don't and the point is 5. $12 would go on six and $12 would go on eight. If the shooter suddenly rolls 7, then the total win (after losses) will be $6. It's not ideal, but, hey, that's gambling and you're ahead. If the shooter rolls the point it won't affect the place bets and you would have lost the don't wager anyway. If the shooter rolls 6 or 8 a few times, the dealer will be giving you money. Just remember that the 7 is more likely than the point. Don't be greedy. Take the place bets down after two or three rolls. The wager on the don't will usually win in the end and then you can savor multiple victories.

Place bets on 6/8 are also fine by themselves or in conjunction with pass and come wagers.

Craps Optimal Strategy

This is it, the Holy Grail for craps. It's the culmination of all the material we've covered to this point. Follow this optimal strategy, and the casino will never have an advantage that exceeds 1.5%.

- Bet the pass, come, don't pass, or don't come.
- Take or lay odds but avoid overbetting.
- Bet the place six or place eight if your gut tells you the shooter will roll a lot of numbers.
- Don't waste time or money on place four, five, nine, ten, or buy and lay bets for the remaining numbers because odds wagers are better.
- Avoid proposition bets and hardways.

A typical pass/come line of play using this strategy would be to bet pass, take odds if a point is rolled and place the six/eight (unless the point is 6 or 8). Aggressive bettors might follow up with one or two additional come bets and odds.

A typical don't-pass/don't-come line of play would be to bet don't pass; take odds if a point is rolled and possibly hedge with the six/eight. Aggressive bettors might follow up with one or two additional don't-come bets and odds.

There is no "wrong" way to combine your bets when you stick to optimal strategy. The only real mistake would be putting too much money on the table or betting on the wrong shooter (if you believe in the effects of setting dice). We'll cover that in the next chapter.

In Review

Combination bets can never outperform the combination's individual components.

Hedge bets that include propositions, hardways, or other high-edge wagers are unprofitable and a waste of money.

The best way to lower the house edge is to make flat bets and take odds.

Place six and place eight are reasonable alternatives to flat bets and odds. The rest of the bets on the table should be avoided (assuming you want the best possible chance for a win).

Craps optimal strategy guarantees the house edge will always be 1.5% or less.

Chapter

What's Your System?

FLIP THROUGH THE BACK PAGES of any gaming magazine or poke around the Internet and you'll find craps systems for sale. "Win money on every number, guaranteed or it's free!" screams one headline. Another one touts, "Our revolutionary system generates BIG PROFITS in either long or short term play." Yet a third promises, "Win over 83 percent of your craps decisions!"

Do you suppose the people selling these systems know craps secrets that have eluded the casinos? Is it possible that two plus one equals four? Of course, all of the above headlines can be technically true. Winning doesn't necessarily mean verified long-term profits, and "big profits" doesn't automatically exclude big losses. As for winning 83 percent of craps decisions, here's how you do it: Bet $10 on the field, $10 place five, and $12 on six and eight.

You will win thirty out of thirty-six decisions. Yup, that's slightly better than 83 percent. That's also an average loss of $28 when you include the other six rolls.

Ouch!

Okay, the magazine and Internet ads don't have the answers. But the questions remain... What should you play? How much should you bet? When should you increase your bets? When should you take wagers down?

Advanced Bankroll Concepts

Most people use a **bankroll** (money set aside specifically for wagering) when they gamble. Unfortunately, the average player doesn't plan much farther than that. The bankroll is treated as a simple **stop-loss**, that is, the gambling stops when the money is gone. **Win-limits** (plans for locking up profits and leaving the table) are nonexistent or vaguely defined. The accounting at the end of the session for the typical player is simply plus or minus, up or down.

Let's say you start a session with $500 and finish with $800. That's a $300 profit. Pretty good, right? But what if I told you that you were up to $2,500 halfway through the session? $300 doesn't sound so good anymore because you lost $1,700!

Here's another scenario: You start a long weekend with $500 and lose it all. That sounds pretty bad. But it's not such a kick in the pants if you were betting green chips ($25 per decision) and

Smarter Bet Tip

It's a good idea to divide your total bankroll into smaller session bankrolls. A session can be an hour, a day, whatever you like. Using a session bankroll prevents you from losing more than a set amount over a specific period of time, so even the worst luck can't wipe out your gambling fun for an entire vacation.

played a total of sixteen hours. The expected loss would be more than $500, depending on your line of play.

Of course, $500 might disappear in five minutes when wagering green chips, but that's beside the point. The size of your bankroll at the end of a session is not necessarily an accurate measure of your overall success or failure. A better indicator of how you did is to look at the amount you risked per wager, the kind of bets you made, and the results of all the decisions.

Knowing your average expected rate of loss is also important (remember that craps is a negative-expectation contest). Optimism aside, the casino has an edge. You're essentially paying a fee (extracted as a portion of your action) to pay for the crew, table, and free drinks. You should know the exact dollar amount of that fee.

Calculating it is the first step to choosing the most profitable line of play for your particular style and temperament.

AVERAGE EXPECTED LOSS

The formula in this section is based on a system that casinos use to determine your expected loss (for comp calculations), but my formula is more accurate then the casinos' version because they assume you're betting the numbers, the field, and occasional propositions. But you're not, right?

How much do you have on the table on average during the second roll of the dice after a come out? Do not include odds. Divide that number by half. That's your expected hourly loss. If you're doing better than that, then you're beating 1.5%. Consider any loss up to that amount as a cost of doing business, or as an entertainment charge.

For those of you who are sticklers for exact numbers, here is the complete computation.

(average total bet x 30 line decisions per hour) x 1.5% = average expected hourly loss

The long version produces a slightly lower number.

Keep in mind that this is an average, a standard for measuring your performance. You'll do a lot better in some sessions and much worse in others. But knowing your average expected loss is helpful when you eke out a small win on big action because you know exactly how much more the casino actually lost in expected revenue, and it's also nice to know what part of a losing session wasn't bad luck but simply a cost of playing the game.

ROLLING STOP-LOSS

A **rolling stop-loss** is a more sophisticated method of handling stop-losses and win-limits than the typical "stop when you lose it all" rule. It also prevents the disappointment of being significantly up and then losing it all back.

A rolling stop-loss can be any amount you choose, and there are various ways of calculating it, but the "sliding window" is pretty typical. Let's say I start a session with 200 units and my window is 100. If I win 50 then the window slips forward by that amount. The original stop-loss was 100 units remaining on the rail (200 – 100 = 100). The new stop loss has moved forward to 150 on the rail (250 – 100 = 150). I will always exit the session if I lose 100 units from the highest point of my bankroll. When my winnings go beyond 100 units (300 units sitting on the rail) then I'm permanently in the black.

Again, for those of you who are sticklers for the math, this system works by limiting action and bankroll volatility. It's

Smarter Bet Tip

One alternative to a rolling stop-loss is a once-through method of wagering. You risk each unit (or group of units) exactly once. A net loss ends the session. A net win is divided into thirds. The original bankroll and one-third of the win is permanently set aside. The remaining money is wagered again using the once-though method.

a practical way of managing your money when playing a negative expectation contest, but it doesn't change the house edge. Wager-for-wager you won't win any more or less on average than someone who never stops playing until the bankroll is exhausted, but if losing is in your future, you'll go there slowly.

Some people have a rolling stop-loss of three. That's right, three. One craps player I know buys in for five or ten black chips ($100 units). He bets one unit per pass and slowly increases if he's winning. His rule is "three lost bets and I'm out of there."

Why buy in for $1,000 if you never expect to lose more than $300? That's a comp game some people play with the casino. They buy in big and bet big, but conservatively. That garners them a better comp rating.

Remember, it's easy to be confused or overwhelmed in the heat of the action. A rolling stop-loss can help you exit with a win.

The downside to having a narrow stop-loss window is that a session can end abruptly. That's not necessarily a bad thing, but it's not automatically good either. Keep in mind that there is a direct relationship between the size of your stop-loss and the total amount you can lose or win. In other words, limiting your losses also limits potential profits because you cannot predict when the dice will tumble your way.

The ideal stop-loss is one that matches your temperament and betting style.

Press or Grind?

Once you've determined your average expected loss/expense and bankroll limits then you can decide how to handle winning wagers. Should you **press** (bet more on subsequent rolls) or **grind** (play ultra-conservatively) and take your profits now?

Smarter Bet Factoid
Famed violinist Niccolo Paganini (1782-1840) loved to gamble, but he wasn't very good at using a stop-loss. On one occasion he pawned his violin to pay gambling debts.

Grinding vs. Pressing

Decision	Grinder's Bet	Grinder's Bankroll	Presser's Bet	Presser's Bankroll
W	1	1	1	1
W	1	2	2	3
W	1	3	3	6
W	1	4	4	10
W	1	5	5	15
L	1	4	6	9
W	1	5	1	10
L	1	4	2	8
W	1	5	1	9
L	1	4	2	7
L	1	3	1	6
L	1	2	1	5
L	1	1	1	4

Grinder is flat-betting single units. Presser is using a 1-2-3 positive progression.

The answer depends on your personality and play goals. Do you want to win a lot of money? The best way to do that is to press. On the other hand, grinding will give you time on the table and a greater probability of squeezing out a small profit. There is no absolute right answer, but here's a side-by-side example of the two approaches.

In this example Presser uses a 1-2-3 **positive progression**. It's a system of raising bets after wins. The player increases the bet by one unit after every win, and then falls back to a single unit after a loss.

This system does very well on streaks, but notice how it loses money on a **choppy table** (alternating wins and losses). Grinder doesn't do nearly as well during the hot streak, but he doesn't lose when the dice go choppy. Keep in mind that the overall frequency of wins to losses in the above sequence happens to favor Presser, but it's just as likely for the table to produce a sequence more favorable to Grinder.

Are you intrigued by positive progressions? There's a world of them out there. One of my favorites is 2-1-2-3-5-8. It wins nicely on a choppy table or on a streak, but its weakness is win-win-lose-lose sequences. You'd be surprised how often those occur.

Note that positive progressions have a dark and nasty doppelganger opposite called **negative progressions** (raising bets after losses). We'll cover those in a later section.

As in the previous stop-loss example, pressing or grinding doesn't change the house edge; it just squeezes or stretches the risk. Some situations become more profitable, while others become more expensive.

For more on positive progressions, check out the *Smarter Bet Guide to Blackjack*.

Smarter Bet Tip
Here are some other positive progressions that you may find profitable: 1-1-2-3-4-5, 2-1-1-2-3-4, 2-1-2-3-4-5, 1-2-2-3-5-8.

Deconstructing the Gambler's Fallacy

Many gambling systems tell you to watch and wait before betting. The theory is that past decisions give you a clue as to what is coming up.

The funny thing is that half of those systems tell you to expect more of the same, and the other half say a change is due.

Consider our coin-flip example from Chapter 1. Let's say the eagle (or the state symbol on a new coin) hits a lucky streak and wins ten consecutive times. What's the probability that the streak will extend to eleven? Should you bet for or against our former commander-in-chief?

Some folks would say that George is "due." Is that right? No. It's not right.

The odds are exactly the same for every flip of the coin.

There are situations when history will affect the future, but in most casino games this is not the case.

Here's why: Deal yourself one card from a deck of cards. You have a 1 in 52 chance of receiving any particular card. Let's say you draw the ten of diamonds. The chance of someone else drawing the ten of diamonds has dropped to zero. In addition, the chance of drawing another red card has dropped to 25 in 51 while the chance of drawing black has increased to 26 in 51. In this situation the first decision (history) will affect subsequent decisions (the future).

Now put the card back and shuffle the deck. The chance of drawing the ten of diamonds is back to 1 in 52. The deck doesn't remember your previous draw.

Another example: spin a roulette ball. Let's say black hits seven consecutive times. Is black now less likely to hit? No. The wheel has no memory.

Dice are the same. Inanimate objects don't respond to history.

Misunderstanding this one truth has cost gamblers more money than all the unfavorable games and poor odds in the entire history of gambling. It's known as **gambler's fallacy**. Gambling systems based on this fallacy are doomed to eventually fail. Why? Because they are not accurately predicting the probability of a win. Bets are increasing (or decreasing) for no valid reason.

Unfortunately, this applies to positive progressions (though they're fun to use) and their dangerous opposites, negative progressions.

The Merciless Martingale

Martingale is the granddaddy of all the negative progressions. Some people swear by the martingale. Most people swear at it. It's usually used in situations when the payout is 1:1 and the true odds are near 50/50. The gambler begins with a base bet, typically one unit. The bet is doubled after a loss. Doubling continues until a win. Then the gambler returns to a one unit bet. The practical effect is a net gain of one unit after every win. Losses have no net effect on the bankroll. It may sound great, but this assumes the final decision in the sequence is a win. That's a big assumption.

The table on page 94 shows how it works.

Remember that the gambler is trying to win it all back plus one unit. So a loss

Smarter Bet Factoid
Don't forget that all craps tables have a limit, so even if a player is tempted to use a negative progression, the larger bets would not be allowed if the system goes too far.

The Martingale

Bet #1	Wager = 1	Net If Win = 1	Net If Loss = -1
Bet #2	Wager = 2	Net If Win = 1	Net If Loss = -3
Bet #3	Wager = 4	Net If Win = 1	Net If Loss = -7
Bet #4	Wager = 8	Net If Win = 1	Net If Loss = -15
Bet #5	Wager = 16	Net If Win = 1	Net If Loss = -31
Bet #6	Wager = 32	Net If Win = 1	Net If Loss = -63
Bet #7	Wager = 64	Net If Win = 1	Net If Loss = -127

at level seven puts the gambler down 127 units. Imagine if the base unit is a ten-dollar bet. Ouch!

But hey, the system only needs one win. What's the possibility of losing seven times in a row?

It's 1 in 128 on a coin-flip-style 50/50 proposition. The true odds are worse (more likely to occur) when playing negative expectation casino games like craps. For example, the odds of seven consecutive losses on the craps pass line are about 1 in 116. Still pretty unlikely, right? Yes, but consider the actual wager. The gambler is risking 127 units against the casino's one unit that seven consecutive losses won't occur. What a dumb bet!

The probability of seeing seven consecutive losses is greater than the probability of winning enough in the interim to cover those losses. Or put another way, the gambler will usually lose 127 units before winning 116. So the martingale is always a long-term loser. It's unavoidable. Yet people continue to use the system. Why?

The biggest reason is that gamblers incorrectly believe the martingale is adjusting wagers up as the probability of winning is increasing. They think that consecutive losses indicate that a win is "due". But guess what? The probability of winning isn't going up. It's exactly the same with every throw of the dice.

As Homer Simpson would say, "Doh!"

Luck vs. Skill

I have a friend who has an adage about craps systems. He says, "You tell me what you're going to roll, and I'll tell you how to bet."

In fact there are some shooters who can indeed do that. They come in two types. First, there are **dice mechanics** who are professional cheats. We'll cover them in a later chapter. The rest do it the legal way. They're known as **golden shooters, rhythmic rollers, hot shooters, golden arms,** and other similarly descriptive names. They operate in the same realm of credibility and reality as psychics. Some people swear it works, and others aren't so sure. Most of these players use a technique that you can use yourself.

Dice Setups

	Numbers										
	2	3	4	5	6	7	8	9	10	11	12
	Ways To Roll										
No Setup	1	2	3	4	5	6	5	4	3	2	1
6-1, 6-1	0	0	1	2	3	4	3	2	1	0	0
6-1, 5-2	0	1	1	2	3	2	3	2	1	1	0
6-1, 3-4	0	1	2	2	2	2	2	2	2	1	0

THE SCIENCE OF DICE

Opposite ends of dice always total 7. Hold a pair between your thumb and forefinger with the sixes on the outside and the ones facing each other. Notice that 2, 3, 4, and 5 are the exposed faces. If you were to toss those dice and they didn't turn sideways, the probability of rolling craps would be zero. The odds of seeing 7 would be 1:3 instead of 1:5. That would be a heck of an advantage on a come-out! Now hold the dice with a six on the outside of one cube and a five on the outside of the other. If the dice don't turn then 7 can be made only two ways, but

6 and 8 can be made three ways. That's an astounding advantage when you're rolling for an inside point.

A setup with 6 on the outside of one cube and 4 on the outside of the other gives all the points an equal chance against 7 (assuming the dice don't turn).

Of course, casinos know all about this. That's why dice are constructed the way they are. The sharp edges are designed to make them catch on surfaces and tumble. The ends of the table are dimpled to make the dice turn when they bounce. And a bounce is required or the results may be declared a no-roll.

And then there's that long toss. Can you loft dice the length of the table without turning them? It can be done, but it takes some practice.

Casinos don't seem to be too concerned about people setting dice because most let you do it. It's no big deal as long as you use one hand and you don't delay the game. It should take about three seconds. Don't make a big show, just flip the

Smarter Bet Tip
Setting dice with the threes angled like a pyramid puts the sixes on the outside and makes the dice less likely to roll craps (assuming the cubes don't turn sideways during the throw).

dice, pick them up, and then pitch them in a way that will reduce a sideways turn.

Does it work? Sometimes yes, sometimes no. Setting dice certainly can't hurt your chances. Betting on someone who sets dice will never be worse than betting on any random shooter.

PSYCHIC DICE AND INTUITION

Why are some players consistently lucky? Is it telekinesis? A psychic connection to the universe? Spend any amount of time at a craps table and you'll experience things that simply defy conventional explanation. One of those things is your intuition. You should listen to it. If you feel an epic roll coming on, then bet the come and take odds. If the table turns cold and you have visions of Darth Vader, then switch to the don't. Remember, you can't make an incorrect bet when following optimal strategy. So just stick to your limits, listen to the universe, and enjoy yourself.

Francisco's System

Francisco Lombardo was a set designer and art director in Hollywood during the 1960s and 1970s (his work includes the TV series *The Man From U.N.C.L.E*). One of Francisco's great joys was to take his twenty-something son Baron to Las Vegas and show him how to play winning craps. Baron would make the bets; Francisco would stand behind him and proudly watch the action. The father and son bonded while the younger man learned the importance of discipline and concentration... lots and lots of concentration.

Francisco wasn't a mathematician, but the system he developed and taught to his son uses an excellent combination of odds and a positive progression to squeeze the maximum amount from a table if the dice are at all willing to give. Be forewarned that Francisco's approach is aggressive. It's not for the faint of heart or for a craps beginner. You should be entirely comfortable at a craps table before using this line of play. Furthermore, this system SHOULD NOT be used unless a player is prepared to risk and lose the *entire session bankroll*. Got that? Okay, here we go.

- Buy in for $1,000.
- Bet the pass and two comes for $15 with double odds.
- Odds are on for all rolls.
- Press all winning flat bets in the following progression: 15-30-45-55-65 (3-6-9-11-13) and continue in $10 increments. Always take double odds.

• Add a come bet if two of the original bets reach level four ($55). Add another come bet if any bet reaches level five.

• Leave the table when a winning streak has ended (two consecutive seven-outs) and you're up at least $1,500, or...

• Leave the table when the bankroll is gone, or...

• Leave the table when you are no longer willing to risk the rest of the bankroll, and your gut says it's time to go.

Baron tells me his father's system once reached $14,000, and it typically produced wins of $2,000 to $4,000. That's not at all surprising since the overall edge was a minuscule 0.61%. There's no doubt that the Lombardos were lucky, but the beauty of this approach is that it doesn't cripple good luck with bad bets. Francisco's system is an excellent way to play aggressive craps on a hot table.

In Review

⚅ **A rolling stop-loss** is a method of managing your bankroll that prevents a substantial loss after a substantial win.

⚅ **Past results** do not affect the current conlest. Inanimate objects do nol have memories.

⚅ **Positive progressions** are fun to use, and they can win you a lot of money in some circumstances, but they don't lower the house edge.

⚅ **Negative progressions** are dangerous and destructive. You should avoid them.

⚅ **Setting the dice** a particular way may help you roll naturals or points more often, assuming you can throw the dice without turning them.

⚅ **Listen to your intuition**, but stick to your limits.

Chapter

Craps Etiquette

IMAGINE A THREE-LEGGED RACE with a dozen contestants tied together. That's craps. The game cannot function unless everyone cooperates. Dealers, stickman, players, and shooter have to be in a rhythm or the whole thing is absolute chaos.

Miscommunication can cause bets to be incorrectly handled or improperly paid. A shooter who doesn't hit the wall can cause a no-roll and delay the game. Ditto for dice that fly off the table. If you ever want to stop a craps game cold, just put one or both hands flat on the layout. A dozen people or more will turn their eyes to you. And you'd better have something important to say.

You shouldn't be intimidated by this need for cooperation, but you should understand that it's an important part of the game. Also understand that some rules are absolute, and others are more like customs or superstitions. The latter may not have a practical basis, but they're rarely broken without some sort of admonishment or minor incident. Think of it like dancing. Even a mosh pit has a routine.

Thou Shalt Not

Every game has some strict rules, like pass interference or roughing the kicker in football. They're a pain, but they're necessary or the game couldn't exist. The following craps rules involve casino security, game integrity, or money-handling procedures. Bending or breaking these dictums will bring warnings from the crew and (in extreme situations) will cause the violator to be ejected from the casino.

Dealers' areas must never be touched. The numbers, the center of the table, and the bank in front of the boxperson are inviolate. Players must never touch them. If a dealer makes a mistake placing a bet, say what you must to call attention to the problem, but don't reach for the chips.

Dice must be thrown correctly. I mentioned this in chapter 2, but it bears repeating here. Use one hand to throw the dice. Do not hold anything else in that hand when you grab the cubes. Do not conceal them from view at any time. Make sure they bounce off the far wall. Do not slam them on the table or grind them in your hand. Aim for the end of the table and try not to knock over stacks of chips.

Money transactions must be secure and observable. Make wagers quickly after the dice have been called. Promptly remove bets from the layout if you don't want them to play. Don't touch bets on the pass line when the puck is on. Never hand money to a dealer. Put it on the layout in a neutral space and ask for change.

A dealer must understand your bet or it is void. Tell dealers exactly what you want, and be sure they understand. If you want an odds bet on the come, mention the number and make sure you say it's odds, as in, "Odds on my four."

All players must have an equal opportunity to shoot. Moving around the table in an attempt to shoot the dice out of sequence is not allowed.

Other no-nos include hanging one's hands over the edge of the rail, resting drinks on the rail, and betting cash (rather than chips) without approval from the boxperson.

Superstitions and Customs

Craps superstitions are so powerful and such an integral part of the game that even some casino bosses believe in them. The house has a clear mathematic edge, but craps is the only game where you'll see a boxperson trying to "break a shooter's concentration" as if throwing the dice was like golf. When a shooter is on a monster roll it often seems that magic has grabbed the table, and even casino supervisors begin to wonder if it will take magic to wrench it back to profitability.

Most craps customs and superstitions involve what supposedly will or will not cause a shooter to pass. Here are some of the most common beliefs and traditions.

A don't bettor increases the chance of a seven-out. Betting against the shooter is tolerated by do players because it's allowed by the rules, but the negative energy is often believed to cause a choppy table or a long string of losses. Don't bettors are not popular at crowded tables. In fact, the stickperson will announce when a don't player is shooting so that do bettors can remove their bets from the layout.

Taking bets down during a pass attempt will cause a shooter to seven-out. This is related to the above negative energy superstition. If you lose faith in the shooter, then his magic may stop working.

Breaking the shooter's rhythm will cause a seven-out. Speaking to the shooter, touching her, or mentioning the word "seven" during a pass attempt is an extreme faux pas. The person is in a zone and must not be disturbed. Here's just one example. Let's say your best friend starts a monster roll while you're away from the table. You approach and realize a hot streak is in progress. The polite thing to do is to stay out of your friend's line of sight and come no closer. The psychic elements that are causing the streak must not be disturbed.

Dice leaving the table will cause a seven-out, unless the shooter continues with the same dice. If one or both of the dice fly off the table, be sure to ask for "same dice" or you'll hear a groan from all the players.

Dice hitting a person's hand will cause a seven-out. Keep your hands off the layout when the dice are flying or the dealers and players will be yelling at you.

A woman who is shooting craps for the first time will always pass, and will likely pass a number of times after that. This is a big one. It may seem sexist, but it is a huge factor in the game. Women who have never played craps are called **craps virgins**, and everyone is looking for the next one. Here's a typical craps virgin story:

> I was at the table once with a honeymooning couple. When the dice came to the woman she didn't want to roll, but every old timer at the table begged her. Finally, the stickman talked her into it. As her pretty young hand reached for the dice I doubled my pass line and bet

a Yo (11)! Sure enough, she rolled a YO! Her next roll was an easy 6. I bet all the boxes, covered all the hard guys, and bet a 12. She rolled a 12. By this time the table was going nuts with bets. She hit a lot of box numbers and then the point number with a hard six. The stick called it the honeymoon special. She blushed when he said it. This went on for about 15 minutes before she rolled the bad number. Everybody was happy! Chips for the players, tips for the crew, drinks for the shooter and her hubby. —Sam Shooter, craps player

In contrast, male craps virgins are often believed to be bad luck. Sorry guys.

Yes, these are just superstitions. But if you're wondering why a chip fill is delaying the game, and the dice are being s-l-o-w-l-y inspected, it's because the boxperson or floor supervisors see the table is hemorrhaging cash, and they're trying to break the shooter's rhythm. This approach also reflects a lingering attitude from the old mob days when bosses looked unfavorably upon "unlucky dealers."

Of course, not all casinos are like this. Many crews understand and accept that streaks are a part of the game, and they'll congratulate a player on her good fortune.

If you find yourself in an establishment that is not so enlightened, don't hesitate to ask for a supervisor or manager and register a complaint. If the situation isn't corrected, you shouldn't play there. Find another place to toss the dice.

Unless of course you believe the superstitions. In that case, I suggest you switch to the don't because the shooter's rhythm has been interrupted.

Tokes

A **toke** is a tip in casino-industry parlance. Ready for a surprise? Casino dealers typically earn half or more of their money from tokes. For example, dealers at MGM Grand in Las Vegas had a total average income of $63,728 and a base pay of $5.35 per hour in 2000. The difference was tokes. But remember, MGM is the largest hotel property in North America (5,005 rooms). Dealers at smaller casinos earn much less, and they depend heavily on the kindness of their customers.

Nobody expects a toke when you're losing, and you should definitely not toke if a game is poorly dealt, but if you have a winning session and the crew made it pleasurable then it's always good form to give something. There are a couple of ways to do this. You can put chips on a neutral portion of the layout and simply say, "This is for the crew." Another way to toke is to bet something for them. "Come bet for the dealers" or "all the hardways for the crew" is always a welcome call.

Not only will your tokes help to support high-quality craps play by encouraging experienced dealers, you'll also find the crew much more accommodating in situations requiring a judgment call that might cost you money. Call it an investment.

In Review

🎲 **Following the rules** is an important part of helping a craps game proceed smoothly.

🎲 **Most craps superstitions** involve actions that will supposedly cause a shooter to pass or seven-out. Speaking to the shooter, touching him, or mentioning the word "seven" during a pass attempt is extremely bad form.

🎲 **Tokes (tips) are the major source** of a dealer's income. It's a good idea to tip if you're winning. Not only is it a nice thing to do, but the goodwill it generates may help your cause in a borderline decision.

Chapter

Safety and Other Practical Issues

CRAPS IS ABOUT HAVING WILD, SPONTANEOUS, UNEXPECTED FUN, but as with most things in life, a little planning and a few precautions will help to insure that all your craps adventure will be pleasant.

This is a necessary part of the game. It's every bit as important as taking odds or hitting the back wall.

So consider this chapter as an addendum to the optimal strategy on page 80. The information here is an integral part of a larger strategy that applies to your entire gaming experience (even when you're not playing craps).

Thwarting Thieves

It's unfortunate, but the mixture of money, confusing noises, tourists in "fun mode," and the constant push of the crowd in a casino create a prime environment for larceny. Purses, wallets, bags, chips, and anything not nailed down or attached to one's body are in danger of disappearing into a mass of pulsing humanity.

Here are some personal safety tips you should keep in mind as you're cheering the shooter.

• Avoid carrying a purse or bag. If you must carry a bag, secure it so that it cannot be opened or moved without you knowing.

• Thieves often use a loud noise or a nearby disturbance to distract attention while they grab unattended chips, cash, or bags. If you hear a loud noise, or you notice a disturbance, first look down and secure your belongings before you look up to see what is happening.

• If someone "accidentally" bumps into you hard enough to knock you off balance, don't worry about who will apologize to whom. Immediately assume you are being robbed. Hold tightly onto anything you want to keep because in the next millisecond it will be forcibly torn from your hand, arm, or pocket. Also, beware when you're "accidentally" doused with a spilled drink. The loud ditzy blonde who is frenetically dabbing your gin-soaked crotch may be covering for a confederate who is scooping up your chips.

Smarter Bet Factoid

When you leave the table a winner it's always a good idea to convert lower denomination chips into fewer easy-to-carry higher denominations. Just put your chips on the layout and ask a dealer to "color up" your winnings.

• Don't toddle upstairs with twenty black chips stuffed in your pocket. Cash out and leave most of it on deposit at the cage. That's the bank-like area of the casino where money transactions are conducted.

• If you must carry a large amount of cash, ask the casino for a security escort. Don't be embarrassed. That's casino security's job. Do it even if you're a tough guy. Anyone can be robbed.

• Don't expect a casino's high-tech wonder toys to help much when someone has stolen your money. Surveillance systems are primarily designed to detect cheating rather than rectify patron-on-patron theft. And the "eye-in-the-sky" only works when a casino can stop criminals in the act. There's not much that can be done after the crime when the criminal has disappeared.

Craps players should be especially diligent because a hot table usually involves a lot of shouting and a throng of people who are elbow to elbow. It's a good idea to keep an eye (or a hand) on your chips to prevent any light-fingered larceny. One popular scam is to squeeze into a tight table and simply scoop off chips when a player is leaning over and not watching.

Another scam involves confusing the dealers and claiming someone else's winning bet. You might think this would be difficult, but remember that a hot table will have many players and dozens of bets working. That's a lot of chips changing hands. Keep an eye on your bets in the heat of the action.

Craps Cheaters

This is a more of a problem for the craps crew than for you, but I'm mentioning it because people who cheat the game are the reason why rules regarding dice and money are so stringent. Dice mechanics will switch dice, slide dice, fix dice, or do any number of other things to unfairly affect the outcome of the throw. It's against the law, and the craps crew is always on the lookout for these criminals.

So the next time you grab the cubes, then lean below the table to put your drink on the ledge, and find yourself surrendering the dice for inspection... well... now you know what it's all about.

Keeping Records

It might sound like a pain, but consistent record-keeping is an important and necessary step to playing an optimal game. Where did the money go? From where did it come? It's impossible to know which tables are busting you and which games are paying for the vacation unless you keep records. Did you make money on the come? Did you lose money playing the field? Is the hedge betting system any better than putting it all on the line? Records reveal all sorts of interesting trends.

Perhaps the worst losses come late at night when you're tired and making incorrect play choices, or perhaps they come early in a session when you're nervous. Perhaps hunger (low blood sugar) causes losses. Conversely, there be might a time or condition when you're a gambling god. Strong coffee on an empty stomach might be a consistent moneymaker. The records will tell you.

And of course, those same records will come in mighty handy if you ever deduct gambling losses on your taxes.

Speaking of taxes...

Gambling and the IRS

Federal taxes apply to all your gambling income, even if a win doesn't reach the W2G threshold for mandatory reporting by the casino to the IRS. The rule is very simple: If you win money; you owe Uncle Sam.

Gambling losses are deductible, but only when they offset gambling profits. And you must keep detailed records of those losses or the IRS will disallow them if you are audited. You'll need to list exactly how much you lost on a particular day at a specific game.

It doesn't need to be fancy. You can do it on any scrap of paper (though it's a good idea to transfer the figures to a spreadsheet or ledger when you get home). Items to record include the date, time, casino, game, machine or table, amount of the buy-in and cash-out, and your net after the session.

Sure, it's a hassle, but remember that this is all about winning. Set aside a few of those green or black chips and buy yourself some excellent professional tax advice.

Smarter Bet Factoid

Record-keeping doesn't have to be complicated. Just carry a pen and piece of paper with you to jot down the basic info: casino, date, time, game, buy-in, cash-out, and length of session. Write those headings down before you go to the casino. You can conveniently transfer the info to a ledger or spreadsheet later.

Craps and the Internet

Craps is one of the few casino games that doesn't translate well to cyber-space. Yes, you can play it on a computer, but Internet craps lacks the camaraderie, mystery, and visceral stimulation that imbue the physical game.

Nevertheless, the Internet provides a craps resource of tremendous value, and that's communication with other players in an international craps community. Here are a couple of resources to get you started.

The Las Vegas Forum at...

http://go.compuserve.com/lasvegas

This is the Internet's first and most comprehensive message board dedicated to the subject of Las Vegas and gambling. It has thousands of messages covering hundreds of subjects, and a large library set aside specifically for craps. The site is hosted by CompuServe, but it's free and available to everyone on the web.

SmarterBet.com at...

http://www.smarterbet.com

This is site dedicated to all of the Smarter Bet Guides. Here you'll get additional information about craps and other gambling games, and you can drop me an e-mail and ask me questions.

And that's it. Now you've got all the tools to play a winning craps game.

Go for it, baby!

In Review

🎲 **Keep an eye on your chips** when the table gets busy. Thieves use confusion as a cover to steal from unwary players.

🎲 **Keep records** of your wins and losses. Records reveal trends that will help you evaluate your play.

🎲 **Federal taxes** apply to all gambling income. Gambling losses are deductible to the extent that they offset gambling winnings, but you must have records of those losses.

🎲 **Check out SmarterBet.com** for more info about craps and other gambling games.

Glossary

action Refers to the relative amount of money wagered in a game. More money is synonymous with more action.

bank craps The version of craps played in casinos. The house banks the action in bank craps. Street or "G.I." craps is played in private venues and is banked by players.

bankroll An amount of money set aside specifically for gambling.

bar the 12 A craps term that indicates which number is a push for a don't bettor on a come-out roll. Some casinos bar the 2 instead of the 12.

big red Slang for 7.

big six/big eight Two sucker bets in craps that are identical in risk to place six or place eight, but only pay even money. Big six and big eight are not allowed in Atlantic City casinos.

box cars Slang for double sixes.

boxperson, boxman The person who supervises a craps game.

buffalo A combination bet that includes the four hardways and 7 (or sometimes 11).

buy bet A craps bet on a particular number. The buy bet wins if the number is rolled before 7. Buy bets are paid at true odds but the casino charges a 5% vig on the amount wagered.

C&E Slang for craps and 11.

cage The bank-like area of the casino where money transactions are conducted.

check or cheque An alternate term for a chip.

choppy table A table with alternating wins and losses.

color up Exchanging chips of a lower denomination for fewer chips with a higher value.

come A wager that wins with a natural or a point, and loses with craps or a seven-out.

come out The first roll for a do or don't bet in craps.

craps A roll of 2, 3, or 12.

craps virgin A woman who is playing craps for the first time.

dice mechanic A cheat who manipulates dice in an unlawful way.

do Any bet that wins with a natural or when a point is rolled.

don't Any bet that loses with a natural or when a point is rolled.

don't pass/don't come A wager that loses with a natural or a point, and wins with craps or a seven-out.

field A craps bet that the next number rolled will NOT be 5, 6, 7 or 8.

gambler's fallacy Refers to the myth that past results affect the current contest.

grind To play conservatively, the opposite of press.

hardway A 4, 6, 8, or 10 thrown as a double.

hop bet A wager that a single number will be thrown in a particular way on the very next roll. See proposition.

horn A combined bet on 2, 3, 11, and 12.

house edge The financial advantage a casino has in a wager. House edge is usually expressed as a percentage. The term is loosely synonymous with vig.

house odds The amount a casino will pay for a winning bet. Not to be confused with true odds. House odds are expressed as an amount that will be paid for an amount wagered.

inside numbers Points 5, 6, 8, and 9.

lay bet A craps bet against a particular number. The lay bet wins if 7 is rolled before the number. Lay bets are paid at true odds but the casino charges a 5% vig on the winning amount.

laying odds A side bet on a don't-pass or don't-come wager made after a point has been established. Odds bets are paid at true odds and have no house edge.

layout The surface of a craps table where bets are placed.

martingale A dangerous negative betting progression in which bets are doubled after each loss.

natural A dice roll of 7 or 11 on the come-out.

negative expectation Refers to a game that takes more in the long run than it pays. Negative expectation games have a house edge.

negative progression A system of increasing bets after losses.

no roll An invalid dice roll, also sometimes referred to as "no dice."

on 1. A bet that is working. Refers to a wager on the table that can be affected by a roll of the dice. **2.** A puck position that indicates a shooter is trying to roll a point.

odds 1. See true odds. **2.** A side bet on a pass, don't-pass, come or don't-come wager made after a point has been established. Odds bets are paid at true odds and have no house edge.

off 1. A craps bet that is on the table but is not working. The dealers and player understand that the money is not at risk. **2.** A puck position indicating the shooter is coming out.

off and on Being paid for one come bet just as another has established a point.

on tilt Playing badly or erratically. A bad mood that adversely affects judgment.

once-through A stop-loss system in which each dollar in a bankroll is risked exactly once.

optimal strategy A system of play that lowers or eliminates the casino's advantage.

outside numbers Points 4 and 10, sometimes including 5 and 9.

pass To roll a natural in craps, or to roll a point before rolling 7.

payoff odds See house odds.

place bet Similar to a buy bet except that the casino takes its vig as a lowered payout rather than as a percent of the wager.

point A number that must be rolled for a player to pass. Rolling the point causes pass-line bets to win and causes don't-pass bets to lose.

positive expectation Refers to a game that pays more in the long run than it takes. Positive expectation games have a player edge.

positive progression A system of pressing (increasing bets) after wins.

press Repeating a bet and increasing the amount after a win.

propositions Any wager that can be decided with a single roll of the dice. One-roll bets in the center of the table are most typically referred to as propositions.

puck A disk (white on one side and black on the other) that is used to indicate the current point.

push A tie; the player doesn't win or lose.

put bet A pass-line bet made after the come-out.

rail The top edge of a craps table.

right Slang for do.

rolling stop-loss A combination of a stop-loss and a win-limit that prevents a player from risking winnings beyond a particular dollar amount.

seven-out Rolling a 7 while attempting to roll a point in craps. A seven-out causes pass-line bets to lose and don't-pass bets to win.

shooter The player who is throwing the dice

snake eyes A dice-roll of 2.

stickperson, stickman The craps dealer who supervises the dice.

stop-loss A plan for exiting a game when a particular amount of money has been lost.

take a bet down Remove a bet from the layout.

taking odds A side bet on a pass-line or come wager made after a point has been established. Odds bets are paid at true odds and have no house edge.

toke Casino industry jargon for a tip (gratuity).

true odds The true probability of winning or losing a contest. Not to be confused with house odds.

vig Short for vigorish. A fee charged to players by the casino. Vigorish is also loosely synonymous with the house edge.

whirl A one-roll proposition bet combining a horn bet with any 7.

win-limit A plan for exiting a game when a particular win goal has been reached.

working bet A bet that is active or on. A wager that can win with a roll of the dice.

wrong Slang for don't.

yo Slang for 11.

Index

Page numbers followed by *f* and *t* indicate figures and tables, respectively.

Acknowledgments

Thanks to Conrad Kageyama for his thoughtful questions, comments, and advice; Ron Luks for helping spread the word; Terry K. Gutierrez, Tim Keech, Bill Gerhart, Winkster, and Baron Lombardo for excellent craps stories; Fay Nestor for her loving support. Special thanks to my editor Sharyn Rosart. Her determination made the Smarter Bet series possible. Thank you also to the designer, Lynne Yeamans.

About the Author

Basil Nestor is an author, journalist, columnist for *Casino Player* magazine, and creator of *CompuServe's* advice series *Ask the Gambling Expert*.

As a television editor and producer, he worked with CBS, NBC, CNN, PBS, and other networks. Basil created the award-winning documentary *Casinos in the Community*, an in-depth report on the gaming industry in Atlantic City. He also produced *Riverboat*, a television program that reveals how gaming is changing the Midwest. Basil has authored six books (including *The Unofficial Guide to Casino Gambling*) and dozens of articles for *Casino Player* and other magazines. Basil is also a frequent contributor to *CompuServe's Las Vegas Forum*.

Got a gambling question? Visit *SmarterBet.com* and send Basil an e-mail.